D0041591

IS IT ReaL?

by H. S. Vigeveno

A Division of G/L Publications
Glendale, California, U.S.A.

New Testament Scripture quotations from
The New Testament in Modern English by
J. B. Phillips, 1958. Used by permission
of the Macmillan Company.
Old Testament Scripture quotations from
King James Version.

Published by
Regal Books Division, G/L Publications
Glendale, California 91209, U.S.A.

Library of Congress Catalog Card No. 70-161386
ISBN 0-8307-0108-7

Is it real? All this talk of God and Jesus?
Is it necessary? This business of a cross and an empty tomb?
Can I trust it? The Bible and the "sweet-by-and-by" some Christians look for?
Isn't religion and church a crutch for people who can't make it on their own?
Is there an answer for the here-and-now?
If questions like these sound familiar,
if you want answers for yourself or your friends,
then this book is for you—and for them!

Contents

A teaching and discussion guide for use with this book is available from your church supplier.

Is It Real?

It often looks as though people don't give a hoot. They're really not interested in Christianity. They approach it with a bored "so what?"

"If *you* want to be religious," they say, "OK. Be religious. But leave me alone. I'm happy. I really couldn't care less."

And yet I'd like to suggest that beneath that bored facade always lies a suppressed hunger. Suppressed and covered over, but a hunger nevertheless—a desire to discover the meaning of life. You see it in the movies and dramas and literature of the times, in our frantic pursuit of materialism and pleasure, as well as in the compulsion to escape boredom and loneliness. And—who is really finding happiness or peace in this world's counterfeit paradise?

"What's it all about? Why are we here? Where are we going? If there is a God, how can we find him?" These are nagging questions that press us from within.

Of course you don't hear people asking "How can I find God?" (That only happened once to Jesus Himself!) You only hear the superficial kind: "How's the stock market doing? . . . What's for dinner? . . .What's the weather going to do this weekend? . . . Where can I find a parking place around here?" (Later on I'd like to explain why we suppress the real questions!)

But let's face it. There isn't a person who hasn't asked about meaning, purpose or God. The cards are stacked against us. As created beings we *have* to know where we came from, what we're doing here and where we're going. Try as we may, we can't seem to bury it beneath layers of indifference or sophistication.

These questions I'm writing about have come from many conversations with skeptics and Christians alike. In small discussion groups and in personal conversations about Christianity, people from all walks of life and differing backgrounds have confronted these issues.

I've written in a conversational style, giving the questions as they were often asked, and discussing them in simple language. It is my sincere hope that this book may be the means of some finding their way to Christ, and so to life.

When these conversations were broadcast in Southern California, there were many encouragements that they be put into print. People wanted them not only for themselves, but to give to friends and relatives. My thanks to all those who so encouraged me.

But especially do I wish to thank those who have earnestly and honestly searched for the truth in many unforgettable conversations. I cherish these talks with them. And to all of them—and they know who they are—this little book is affectionately dedicated.

H. S. Vigeveno
Hollywood, California

CHAPTER 1

Conversation with an Atheist

I've talked with you many times. And frankly, it's always a pleasure. We've had lunch together, we've sat in your front room, or we've talked in my office. And whether you were a college student, a working girl, a distinguished businessman, a laborer, a busy but questioning housewife or a person uprooted and passing through a critical period, you generally broach the subject like this:

"I hope you won't mind if I'm perfectly frank with you, but . . ."

I always have to assure you that I'm not in the least bit offended by what you may tell me. That takes you by surprise, because you've talked to Christians before, and some of them got very upset with your views.

Sometimes you say: "You know, I have difficulty believing in God. I suppose you're shocked to hear me say this, but I just can't believe. Perhaps you'd call me an atheist. I don't know. When I was younger, I believed. But I've done a lot of thinking. I've come to the conclusion that religion is really not necessary. You can be a good person without believing in God."

1

I understand. And I agree that there are good-living people, ethical people who don't believe in God, or who aren't especially religious. Still that doesn't prove anything.

But you're just beginning: "Take modern science," you continue. "It's proven that the Bible is wrong. The story of creation in the Bible is too simple. Evolution teaches that we came from the animals through a process of thousands of years, millions of years perhaps. Who knows? So, I don't see why you need God for that."

And then we've talked about evolution. I've stopped being amazed at the fact that you really haven't thought it through. You think that evolution is opposed to God. Either one or the other. That's too simple.

Have you ever listened to the intelligent position of any theist (and I don't have to tell you that a theist is a person who believes in God)? I don't deny the possibility of evolution: that is, for example, that animal life precedes human life. We didn't all get here on the same day. (That's not to admit that man came from the monkey. You didn't, did you?)

Incidentally, the Bible follows the scientific pattern from vegetation to sea life to animals to man. Or should I say evolution follows the biblical pattern? If the Bible had put man here *before* the animals, you'd really have a case. It doesn't make that mistake.

Neither do I set dates for the creation. I know there are some Bibles that carry a date in the margin of 4004 B.C. That was the day Adam got here. But that isn't actually *in* the Bible. Some bishop guessed at it. His name was Ussher, and if you won't mind the pun, we'll usher him right out of our conversation. He was completely mistaken.

Creation may have taken millions of years. The Bible

2

doesn't say "when." But how did it get started? Where did life come from? That's the real question.

"Well," you say, "it may have come from elements or molecules coming together."

Where did the molecules come from?

"Well, you're getting back to where the earth came from. The earth probably was a spark from some other planet."

Where did that planet come from?

"From other elements."

Where did they come from?

"Well . . ."

You see, we're just going farther back to the very beginning of things. And here the Bible calls a halt and states in utter simplicity: "In the beginning *God* created. . . ."[1] God had a hand in creation all along, particularly in the creation of man. With man He brought something altogether new into being. The Hebrew word indicates a creative act. It's the same word used to describe the creation of earth.

"I just can't believe it. I still can't believe there is a God. Why is it all necessary?"

Did you know that Darwin, the father of evolution, with his precise, scientific mind said: "If we consider the whole universe, the mind refuses to look upon it as the outcome of chance." The opposite of chance is order, mind, intelligence. We call that "God."

"Anyway," and now you switch on me, "you can't prove there is a God. You can't prove Him to me."

Now, there you've got me. You're right. I can't prove Him. Sure, I can parade out some of the old arguments. It's been done before. You want me to try? You want to know what I might have to say? All right. I'll list a few, and keep it simple.

First of all, there's that old Aristotelian logic about *cause*. I pulled that on you a moment ago, when I sug-

3

gested that the ball had to start rolling somewhere. Cause, mind, intelligence, God—the prime mover, the first cause. As the Bible says, "In the beginning God. . . ."

Secondly, consider the argument that you can't get something out of nothing. *Matter cannot create itself.* No table, chair, car or computer ever yet made itself. Everything speaks of purpose and design. As a watch argues for a watchmaker, so earth and matter and man point to a purposeful Creator. Even your reason, your mind is a gift!

Then there is our innate sense of *right and wrong.* Where did we get it? Where did it come from? The need for fair play; our conscience; a standard of morality. If we reject God, we accomplish it by using our sense of right and wrong. The Bible asks persuasively: "He that planted the ear, shall he not hear? he that formed the eye, shall he not see?"[2]

Finally, what about *religious experience?* Can you be sure that those who claim to have experienced God were all mistaken? Suppose you were the only person who saw the sun rise today. Then, maybe, that could have been a delusion. But what if thousands saw it also?

Well, I could continue, but again I admit that I cannot prove God to you. For if I could, somebody else would have done it before me! And that means no one would be an atheist any longer! When Galileo proved that the world was round, there weren't any arguments. Only a fool would think it's flat.

"Why can't you prove God like that?"

If God can be proven to exist, He becomes the product of my reasoning. God is reduced to a scientific proposition which man demonstrates. Then man has limited the limitless, and made the Eternal the work of his own mind. Tennyson once wrote that "nothing worthy proving can be proven, nor yet disproven."

4

"Ah, now you're talking my language. You Christians say that God has made man in His image. I say, man has made God in his image. It is all the product of your mind. You've created your own God."

You know, you're allowed to come up with that, because you have been given the freedom to affirm or deny God. I say I can't prove God to you. Let me ask you: Can you disprove Him? Can you demonstrate conclusively that God does not exist?

Actually, doesn't your position leave you in an awkward spot? A person who believes in God points to God as the Creator of all things. What do you say? You throw up your hands and raise your eyebrows. You don't know. Who knows? Who cares? I, for one, don't think that sounds either logical or intelligent.

Suppose I eat and drink and feed myself, but give no thought to where food comes from, what it is, or how it is produced. It's not important, I say. All I need to do is eat. I buy it at the market, I know it's good for me, but I never bother to think of how it got there, where it came from or who may be responsible for it all.

You see the point?

So where does that leave us? If God cannot be proved (or disproved) by logic and reason, then He must be comprehended in other ways. Would you believe: *faith*? I know that doesn't sound very brilliant or original.

By faith I do not mean something contrary to reason, as though faith is like a cup of tea and reason a cup of coffee. No real connection in substance. That's not my cup of tea, you say? Look at it this way. Faith moves beyond reason. It overreaches the boundaries of logic.

When you're out for a swim, there's a point beyond which you cannot go. It's your limit, your point of endurance. So it is in the realm of knowledge. There are

5

limits for man, boundaries beyond which he is unable to move. Would it make sense to you that God is *beyond* these limits? Then only by faith can we reach Him.

Or, picture reason like a circle. Then picture faith as a straight line which cuts through, and then goes out of that circle. Faith ventures into that realm where God is no longer an idea of the mind, but real, living, true!

Carl Sandburg tells about the white man who drew a small circle in the sand and humbled the red man: "This is what the Indian knows." Then he drew a circle around the small one, proclaiming: "This is what the white man knows." The Indian then grabbed the stick and swept an immense ring around both, saying "This is where the white man and the red man know nothing!"

Look at the way the Bible defines faith: "Now faith means putting our full confidence in the things we hope for; it means being certain of things we cannot see."[3]

Do you see what faith means? It is an inner confidence in something beyond the realm of human knowledge. It extends to the invisible. It is not bound to the rational, but pushes off for the experimental, the real! This applies not only to the future but also to the past:

"It is after all only by faith that our minds accept as fact that the whole scheme of time and space was created by God's command—that the world which we can see has come into being through principles which are invisible."[4] How else can we approach such questions?

Thomas Edison said: "We don't know the millionth part of one per cent about anything. We don't know what water is. We don't know what light is. We don't know what gravitation is. We don't know what electricity is. We don't know what heat is. We have a lot of hypotheses about these things, but that is all."

6

So, if you want to find God, faith is essential: "The man who approaches God must have faith in two things, first that God exists and secondly that it is worth a man's while to try to find God."[5]

"But what if I don't have faith? How can I believe in God without faith?"

How do you learn about love? Not by letting Freud analyze it or hearing some singer emote about it. But by experience. Faith isn't something that just comes to you. Nor is it something some people have and others don't. The way to begin is to believe that it *may* be so. Be willing. That's all anyone can ask of you. You can't make yourself "have faith." But you can be open, open to experience, open to love, open to God.

The great Russian novelist, Leo Tolstoy, tells in his confession how he vacillated between joy and despair. Not once or twice, but hundreds of times. He tried to convince himself of God.

"There is no God," he said to himself. "Nothing. No miracles can prove him. Nothing is as real as my own life."

And then he asked himself: "But my conception of God, where did it come from? I should long ago have killed myself if I did not hope to find him!"

And so, slowly, surely, dawned the conviction and the reality by faith—"and I began to live!"

I don't expect you to believe so quickly, but wouldn't faith be better than imprisoning yourself in a limited circle of scientific knowledge? Think about it. I know you will.

Notes

[1]Genesis 1:1
[2]Psalm 94:9
[3]Hebrews 11:1
[4]Hebrews 11:2
[5]Hebrews 11:6

CHAPTER 2

So You're an Agnostic

So you've been thinking: "Maybe it will make you feel good, but you scored a little with me." (Who would feel good about that sort of success?)

"You made me think. I can't be a complete atheist. I mean, there has to be some explanation for the universe, the world, for man and all that. A person who believes in God at least has some answers. An atheist doesn't have *any*."

Go on.

"I read somewhere that Bertrand Russell, the philosopher, was asked to explain how he thought the world began. He only replied, 'It's just there, that's all.' That left me with a blank, a void, nothing—you know? Even the Greeks believed in a first cause and you were say-

8

ing matter can't create itself. So, as I say, I've been thinking about it."

Keep talking.

"Maybe there is a God. I don't know. I'm saying 'maybe.' Now, what difference does it make? I know I asked that before, but I want to know. Isn't it important how you live? To me living seems more important than believing. Like they say, what you are speaks so loud I can't hear what you say."

You have something there. I must agree with you—of course it's important how you live. Only don't overlook this simple fact: What you believe determines how you live. Not the other way around. If you believe you have the right to take your own life, you might commit suicide. If you don't, it's not likely you will.

If you believe in justice and decency you'll live accordingly. Or at least, you'll try! If you don't think morals matter, you won't. A belief in God should influence your living. I'm sure it ought to have far more effect on many Christians, but would they actually be better if they had *no* faith?

"OK. Even if I buy that—and I'm not sure I can—what about this 'faith'? What if you don't have faith? I don't. How can I know God?"

Well, you're an agnostic now, a person who says that there may be a God but who doesn't know Him. There are many honest people like yourself. I enjoy talking with you, not only because of the challenge, but because there's something genuine about you. So let's get into it, since you never abandon one form of life for another unless you have a good prospect, unless you have something else to stand on.

I want to ask you, what kind of an agnostic are you? There are two kinds. That startles you? You thought there was only one type? Here's what I mean. There is the person who says he doesn't know God and nobody

9

else knows either. Then there's the one who admits he doesn't know God, but is open to the fact that perhaps others have experienced Him. Now which are you?

"Suppose I say that I don't know and nobody else knows either?"

Do you really want to make that sweeping a statement? If you do, you will hardly be motivated to seek God. An agnostic who says that nobody else knows God, tends to remain closed. An agnostic who admits others may have experienced God will at least be open. See how what you believe influences your action or inaction?

You deplore bigotry, don't you? I know you do. And yet your position is bigoted if you dare to affirm that no one else has ever known God. How can you answer for Moses, David or Jeremiah? For Augustine, Teresa or St. Francis? For Luther, Wesley or Livingstone? For that matter what will you make of this remark by Jesus, which He made to a group of religious people: "I know him, and if I said I did not know him, I should be as much a liar as you are! But I do know him and I am faithful to what he says."[1]

Sure, some people lie about it. Those to whom Jesus was talking were not telling the truth. But what about Jesus Himself? Did He lie about it too? With all you know about Him, does He sound like a cheat? If He were bluffing, He was a fraud. If He told the truth, He really knew God. It comes down to that.

"But I'm not Jesus."

True. What about His apostles? They were ordinary fellows; fishermen, tax gatherers, laborers. They spoke of knowing God. And so have many Christians throughout the years.

"All right, then, what if I'm an agnostic who doesn't know God, but I admit—with some hesitation—that others have found Him. What good does that do *me?*"

10

At least, now you're an honest agnostic. You're not bigoted or intolerant. You're willing to hear others, and that means you'll listen to what they have to say. The clean truth may keep tugging at your sleeve—if they've found Him, why can't I?

"OK, I'll listen. But you're not going to tell me that all the people in church have experienced God, are you? Maybe a few here or there, but most of the church people I know are hypocrites. You can't trust them. I knew a man who was very active in church. He was an official and ushered, and he always talked about Christ. He ran a shoe repair place. I took some shoes to him once. Once—that's all. That was enough. He did a terrible job. When the soles came off in a couple of weeks, I went back to him and showed him. He shrugged his shoulders and said I must have caught them on something. If that's Christianity, you can have it. And if you're going to tell me that I've got to believe that church people have found God, forget it. I won't buy it."

I don't blame you. Most everybody I know has a story like that about some Christian who doesn't act like a Christian. I'll admit there *is* hypocrisy in the church, and there are many Christians who don't behave as Jesus taught. But is that really a good excuse? Is it enough of a reason to remain an agnostic? Or default on an experience of God? Let's shelve this whole subject for another time, when we can talk about the church and hypocrisy and all that.

"Wait just a moment," you say, and I can see that you're really wound up now, "if you're going to tell me the church has the answer, just think of all the wars the church has fought or sanctioned. What about the Crusades? Those bloody battles? Is that what Jesus taught?"

I can't defend the Crusades, although those men

must have believed in a cause for which to fight, wrong as it may have been. I can't defend those bloody battles either. And it wasn't what Jesus taught. But again I think we've gone off the subject. Let's talk about all of this when we can discuss the church itself. I promise to get into it, then.

We're now talking about agnosticism. How can I find God? That's our question. Now here's Robert Frost, the American poet, saying, "Don't be an agnostic. Be something." What do you make of that?

"Robert Frost to the contrary," you reply, "I think I'm trying to be something, to live for something. I still want to know how I can find God. If He is to be found, why is it so tough for people like me? Why doesn't God just come up to me, tap me on the shoulder and say, 'Here I am'? Then I'd believe. You bet I'd believe."

That's a good way of putting it. I guess it wouldn't make much sense to remain an agnostic if God tapped you on the shoulder and told you to believe in Him. But, strange to say, even this kind of evidence doesn't convince some people.

When Moses went into Egypt before Pharaoh, he showed him miracles and signs from God. He told Pharaoh that he came in the name of the Lord God. Pharaoh *saw* the evidence. There were plagues and signs and wonders. Sometimes he'd soften, and then he'd harden again. He refused to let the Israelites go. Finally, he sent them out of the land following a terrible plague. Then he stiffened again, pursued them, and drowned in the Red Sea, proud and obstinate.

There are those who, in spite of overwhelming evidence, refuse to believe. Evidence and proofs are never sufficient. You wouldn't be like that? Perhaps not. Pharaoh is an extreme example, I admit.

But then there are others like Julian Huxley. This

12

modern philosopher feels a relief not to have to deal with God; that is, a God whom we can know. "It's a great relief," he says. Naturally it is. There's really no danger about holding to the "Absolute" or accepting an "Infinite Mind." You don't have to worship it. Better yet, you don't have to obey it.

"I read in a book by Peter de Vries," you now tell me, "where one of the characters says something like this: 'If you want my opinion on the mystery of life, here it is in a nutshell. The universe is like a safe to which there is a combination—but the combination is locked up in the safe.' Now to me that makes a lot of sense."

I see. Is it a relief to assume this mystery is locked up in a safe? So "it" can't bother you? It seems to me that if you conceive of God in this way, you will never attempt to know Him. You won't make the effort, and worse, you will refuse to believe that *He's* made any effort, either! Why should He bother to come out of the safe?

I prefer Einstein's reverent statement that "ideas come from God." "God is subtle, but He is not malicious," was his credo. By this Einstein meant that a scientist (a man) could expect to find his task difficult, but not hopeless.

But suppose I change the picture. Suppose I say— God is *love*. Now, you can keep Him locked up in a safe? Love is reality. Love is essence. Love is life. And love always makes an effort to communicate. I realize this is taking you a bit too far for the moment, but do you see what I'm driving at? There's a vast difference between God as mere "Idea," locked up in a safe, and the Christian affirmation that "God is love."

Now I admit we certainly don't know everything about God. We are a little like fish in the ocean. They know about their immediate surroundings (I presume)

13

but what do they know about the currents, the tides, the world about them or the universe for that matter? Nothing. We do have better brains than fish, but what do we actually know of the "Almighty"? of "Providence"? or even of "Infinite Mind"?

Do you remember Hamlet's speech: "There are more things in heaven and earth, Horatio, than are dreamt of in your philosophy"?[2]

Moses put it this way: "The secret things belong unto the LORD our God: but those things which are revealed belong unto us and to our children for ever, that we may do all the words of this law."[3] There are great mysteries. Much remains hidden. But there is also revelation. What we may know is discoverable, not only by reason or logic, but through faith.

Notice this. Faith, in this sense, is a response. It is not simply our venturing, our hoping, our desire to believe something. It's a response to the God who has come toward man. What revelation? That brings us to Jesus. He is the revelation of God—of the love of God.

"The love of God? Now there's something that throws me completely. How can you talk about the love of God when there is so much suffering in the world? Six million Jews killed in gas ovens and a God of love?"

I know that raises many questions. However, we must reserve that for a special session, later, when we can talk about suffering. For now, let me put it this way—only because of Jesus, do Christians declare they know God.

Here's why. The New Testament asserts: "It is true that no one has ever seen God at any time. Yet the divine and only Son, who lives in the closest intimacy with the Father, has made him known."[4]

No one has seen God. But is that proof God cannot reveal Himself? I quoted Hamlet a moment ago. Where

14

is Shakespeare in *Hamlet,* or in any of his other plays for that matter? You learn about him, to be sure, but Shakespeare himself you can't find. Does that mean he doesn't exist? Of course not.

What if there were a play in which the author introduces himself, and a little like Alfred Hitchcock making a personal appearance in his films, comes on stage? Only in this play the author is pelted off the stage as an imposter by the players?

That's exactly what happened. The God who loves man has made a personal appearance on the stage of our world. And we got rid of Him!

Only God can reveal God.

Faith is a response to that revelation, a response which can take you through the realm of human knowledge into the experience of God. Maybe those are just *words* to you, inadequate as they are to convey *meaning.* But look. If there are those who have experienced God, then it remains a possibility for you, too!

Be open to it. Jesus said: "Ask and it will be given to you. Search and you will find. . . . The one who asks will always receive; the one who is searching will always find."[5]

The one who is searching will find. *Always.*

Notes

[1]John 8:55
[2]*Hamlet,* Act I, Scene 5
[3]Deuteronomy 29:29
[4]John 1:18
[5]Matthew 7:7,8

CHAPTER 3

But Whose God?

Now let's get to your next big question. Sometimes you state it like this:

"If we're going to thrash out this question of God, I want to know *whose* God? How can I know which God to believe in? The African believes in one God. The Hindu in another. Jews and Christians don't agree. So, who's to say which one is right?"

You have a good point. There are many different names for God, although some have tried to prove that whether you call Him Allah, Krishna or Jehovah, it's all the same; there is only one. If this is true it would make no difference whether you belong to one religion or another. But it does make a difference. I'll explain what I mean.

Let's begin by dividing the religions of man into

two. Some religions teach the discovery of God or truth or whatever they choose to call the Eternal. Others believe in revelation. Now here's the disparity.

The major religions of the East follow the path of discovery, (Hinduism, Buddhism, Confucianism, Taoism, Shintoism, etc.). They suggest such methods as meditation, yoga, exercises for the body and mind, good deeds, prayers, and avoiding suffering. Many teach the endless cycle of reincarnation, which means man proceeds to purification through many lives. The point to remember is that all these religions attempt to reach up to God. They do not teach God reaching down to man.

Revelation, on the other hand, is a movement *down*. Revelation is given to man. God makes Himself known. God reveals Himself. He shows what He is like. Most Western religions, as we know them, teach God's disclosure of Himself.

Here, then, you are forced to make a choice between a religion of discovery and a religion of revelation. You cannot have both. If I were to show you a box and ask you what was in it, you could take the lid off and say, "Oh, I see!"—you discovered it. But suppose *I* took the lid off and showed you, that would be revelation. You can't have it both ways. Once I've revealed the contents, you don't have to discover any more. You know.

When it comes to God, we say man *cannot* discover Him. There's no lid to remove from the universe. God must reveal Himself. And that's precisely what He has done.

Now, if God has revealed Himself, we need only to find out how He did it. When? Where? In what manner? If we snub that revelation and try to climb the ladder of discovery by ourselves, that would be like trying to learn to fly while bypassing the invention of the airplane. (That's been attempted, of course!)

17

"All right," you say, "suppose God has revealed Himself. I'll try to go along with it. But which God? My question still remains. If Jews and Christians and, I don't know how many others, believe in this revealed God, who is right? The Jews believe in one God and the Christians in a Trinity."

I do understand your confusion. At least at this point you realize the difference between discovery and revelation. As to which so-called revealed religion is right, that's something else again.

Some religions teach that revelation is in a book, others in the law and others through an inspired prophet. Only Christianity declares that God Himself took on human flesh and revealed Himself in person. I'm not asking you to believe this just yet, but I do raise the question—which of these would be the highest type of revelation?

"God coming into the world in person? That's hard to swallow, you know. But why? Can't we know God in nature, in creation?"

Of course God reveals Himself through nature. He has created all things. You look at the moon and the stars and recall the scientist's information that stars stretch out millions of light years away. You cannot conceive of it. Or you take a flight in a jet and look down on the world. You fly over snow-clad mountains or vast prairies and you're overawed. When you think of all the people down there in the cities and contemplate your own little circle, sometimes you just have to stop your brain from thinking any further. Your *brain*. That's another miracle of creation.

Of course God speaks through nature, through the miracle that is you, in all of creation. Just as reading a book gives you some ideas about the author. But it's not enough! You may read a book without choosing to

18

know the author, without even considering him. So often men read the book of nature like that too.

It's not enough. We still don't know what God is like. Is He in the quietness of nature? Or is He revealed in an earthquake, a famine, a crippling hurricane? How can you harmonize the song of a bird with the ferocity of a lion? The tenderness of an infant with the deadly bite of a cobra? Why is all creation "kill or be killed"? What kind of a God allows tarantulas, and deadly viruses you cannot even see, and for that matter (to get quite mundane) the mosquito?

This God leaves too many questions unanswered in nature. . . .

God also reveals Himself in our conscience. We all possess a sense of right and wrong. Even the so-called heathen distinguish between good and bad. An African chief declared: "If someone steals my wife, that's bad. If I steal someone else's wife, that's good." That may not be your sense of values, but it's a kind of conscience nevertheless. Where does that come from?

C.S. Lewis, who was a professor of English literature at Cambridge, was surprised to discover that the Babylonians, the Greeks, the aborigines and the American Indians all denounced murder, treachery and falsehood, while praising kindness, honesty and even mercy over justice. There are certainly differences; yet even savages who cannot count to twenty have ethical standards!

God has revealed Himself to His entire human family. All men have a conscience.

But that's not enough either. Is God good *and* evil, since man is a mixture? Can we project God from what we know of man and his conscience? Hardly!

Even though the entire human family experiences a sense of right and wrong, the world is not good. Man does not follow the golden rule. (You may think that

19

you live according to it, but you probably don't think your neighbors do.) What can we do about our failures? How can we clear our conscience? Our own and the world's? Is there forgiveness? No, it's obvious we need another kind of revelation.

What am I leading up to? Until now we've talked about a universal revelation of God. All men can see something of God in nature, and they have a conscience. We may call this "general revelation." But it is not enough. Therefore God has given us another kind of revelation—"special revelation," not in a book or through a prophet, but in person. Christianity goes all the way. It declares God became man. He lived in our midst.

I know what this sounds like to you, but I want you to understand that this is precisely what Christianity has been saying all along: "God, Who gave to our forefathers many different glimpses of the truth in the words of the prophets, has now, at the end of the present age, given us the truth in the Son."[1] And in case you think this Son is less than God, the passage immediately goes on to say: "Through the Son God made the whole universe, and to the Son he has ordained that all creation shall ultimately belong."[2]

You grasp what this means, don't you? It sets Christianity apart, without hesitation, from all other religions. "I see many religions contrary to one another, and therefore all false, save one," said Blaise Pascal. Moses was a great leader, Buddha an enlightened teacher and Mohammed a prophet. But Jesus is the Son of God—God in human flesh visiting this planet. No other religion even teaches this invasion of God for the salvation of the world.

I know I'm jumping ahead of you at this point. It is impossible to talk about God apart from His self-disclosure in Jesus. Let's just say that *if* this is so

20

(mind you, I'm not telling you that you have to accept it!), *if* this is so, then here would be the supreme revelation of God. A book, a prophet or a code cannot hold a candle to it. Here is the one unique happening in our world. And if it did happen, we would be completely senseless not to pay any attention to it.

It sounds foreign to us, of course. We are used to everyday experiences, observable data, scientific facts. We live in the secular world. Yet we should not discard revelation for this reason. We've moved into a space age, exploring the universe and we've had to make adjustments accordingly.

A television program capitalized on that with an unusual gimmick. It projected a couple of astronauts back through time to prehistoric days. Of course that created numerous comedy situations between the cavemen and those astronauts. In a way we also need to adjust. We're faced with an invasion of God from outer space, and our mundane little minds can't quite comprehend it.

You ask me now: "Is this actually what Christianity teaches? I've never heard it put like that. But how could God possibly become man? Isn't God much bigger than all that? Isn't that bringing God down to our level?"

Perhaps. But look at it this way. Suppose you're walking along the beach, or taking a little boat ride offshore. When you return home at the end of the day, you feel you have experienced the sea. Have you? You haven't sailed across the Pacific or ventured into the Antarctic region through the ice. But you have experienced a *little* of the sea, enough to boast that you know something about it.

Of course God is bigger than man. He is the Almighty, the Creator, the Eternal. But for God to contain Himself in man, to come into flesh, to limit Him-

21

self in order to communicate with us—this does give us an adequate knowledge of God. Just as a little boat ride offshore puts you on the ocean!

"At the beginning God expressed himself. That personal expression, that word, was with God and was God, and he existed with God from the beginning. So the word of God became a human being and lived among us."³ As my words express my thoughts, so God has expressed Himself in Jesus. How else could God do it? We wouldn't understand any other revelation. His majesty would overwhelm us, just as you'd scare an ant or a fly if you'd try to communicate with it.

Consider this conversation Jesus held with His disciples: "If you had known who I am, you would have known my Father. From now on, you do know him and you have seen him," He said.

Philip, one of the twelve then asked Him: "Show us the Father, Lord, and we shall be satisfied."

"Have I been such a long time with you," returned Jesus, "without your really knowing me, Philip? The man who has seen me has seen the Father."⁴

That is either the most amazing statement in all of literature, or else it is sheer blasphemy. You know from history how some of His own people interpreted these words. They called Him a blasphemer. Has history borne out Jesus' evaluation, or theirs?

"Then you believe in the Trinity? You say Jesus is part of God? Is Christianity the only true religion?"

Now, wait a minute. The question of the Trinity we'll tackle some other time. As to Christianity being the only true religion, I'll let you make up your own mind about that. I've merely said that God's great revelation of Himself is not in nature or in conscience, not in a law or a book, but in this Person. You see, we are faced with these words: "the man who has seen me has seen the Father." Either blasphemy, delusion, or truth.

Of course it's hard for us to comprehend. Have you ever tried to train a dog? You point to an object on the floor. The dog merely sniffs at your finger. He doesn't know what you're driving at yet. All he knows is *facts* —a finger is a finger, and not *meaning*—that you're pointing at something!

A cat would be even more exasperating. And humans? As long as we refuse to look for meaning, we'll never consider this revelation of God in Jesus. Neither will we grasp what God intended for us to see.

Now turn it around. Is it possible to expand from the life of Jesus a picture of what God is like? If we magnified man—any man, it doesn't matter whom—and enlarged him as a photographer would blow up a negative, what would we get? A monster, a blurred and confused mixture of good and evil. Certainly no pure God of love.

But if we took Jesus and made this enlargement, expanding it to the infinite, wouldn't it remain quite sharp and accurate? If this begins to make sense to you, don't reject God's self-disclosure until you've investigated it from every side.

Consider what Jesus said: "I myself am the road and the truth and the life."[5] Surely that must be a challenge for you, a challenge to find the truth. But I must give you fair warning. Any response you make to God's revelation will mean a change in your life, just as when you first fell in love, you began to change your attitudes and behavior.

So, here's my question. Are you game for a change?

Notes

[1]Hebrews 1:1
[2]Hebrews 1:2
[3]John 1:1,2,14
[4]John 14:7–9
[5]John 14:6

CHAPTER 4

Why Does God Allow Suffering?

"Whenever I think about God, one question keeps popping up in my mind. It really troubles me. Why is there suffering in the world? Why is there so much misery? Why does God allow it? Why are there earthquakes and hurricanes? Why does God permit war? Why is there mental illness and cancer and untimely death? Why do innocent children suffer? Why are some born blind or lame or have to go through life with the mentality of a four-year-old? Is this fair? How can you possibly harmonize this with God—let alone with a God of love?"

Now you've raised *the* question. It's the one question I've heard most often. I suppose it's baffled man from the beginning of time. But this one little word *why* can do mortal damage to us. It may lead us into doubt and confusion.

Men have done their best with this problem, but it's been like hacking away at an iceberg, hoping it would melt and simply disappear. But it hasn't melted, and chipping off a few pieces here and there hasn't helped either. Not enough anyway. Still, the only thing to do is attempt an honest answer.

But before I do, I want to raise another question, which is like a countermove in chess. It's calculated to throw you off balance temporarily. Why does it *have* to be answered? Why must we know? Why does man shake his fist at God, daring Him to give an explanation of His world? What does this tell you about man? That he is curious? Yes. That he demands an answer? Surely. That he wants to know how God can be loving when all the facts shout otherwise? Of course.

But if we consider the world cruel or unjust, where did we get this idea? (I raised that argument before, remember?) You don't call a line crooked unless you have some notion of what's straight. You don't question suffering unless you have some concept of love and perfection—which, obviously, has been given you by the God whom you fight and question!

Man, created by God, is restless (as Augustine said so long ago) until his heart rests in God. The cards are stacked against us. We may deny God, but we seek Him nevertheless.

And, since I brought that up, do you mind if I make another move to clarify man's argument with God? When man fails in his search, he creates his own gods. That explains all the idolatry you read about in history, and it also throws light on the idolatry of our times— materialistic pursuits, the lust for things, sex, prestige, pleasure. Anything to fill the void.

All right. Let's get to the point. How can God allow

suffering? You may ask: "Do you think it has anything to do with punishment?" I'm sure you don't think so.

"I don't. But I've heard many religious people talk that way."

You're right. Some religious people have a simple answer: "It is the will of God." That only sends people like you frantic. "How can it be the will of God? How can a good God allow something evil, something hideous?"

What these people are talking about (at worst) is that everything is the will of god. They include all disasters, earthquakes, accidents, illness, war, death. (I don't buy that.) And what they are talking about (at best) is that they have discovered the will of God in their own suffering. I'd like to clarify that.

Christians find a purpose in the test through which they are forced to live. Suppose they lose an only son at an early age. No one should say to them that this son, whom they loved so much that at times it was painful, had been taken from them by God's will. That would be cruel and anything but comforting. But they themselves after great sorrow, much prayer and deep reflection may believe it to be the will of God. *They* see it that way. They knew their son was young enough to be simple, pure, innocent and in his childlike way loved God. And in accepting it, they drew close to God.

Two missionaries lost their only daughter from leprosy. They could very well have rebelled at God serving them this way. How could He do it? They didn't. They established one of the world's largest leper asylums. Their daughter's death opened the door for thousands. Was there a purpose?

Or consider the young man whose brilliant and great future was interrupted by cancer. "Nothing before," he said, "*nothing* would have brought me to my senses. But now that I have found God, it is worth it all."

But we have jumped ahead. This is only one explanation, to see suffering as within the purpose of God. Yet it must never be made from the outside as an observation, but from within as experience. From the outside it's a judgment; from within it can become healing.

"But can we return to the question?" you ask. "Why does a God of love allow suffering? Suppose a drunk runs over an innocent child. Is that God's will? Why should that child die or the parents suffer? Furthermore, if God is all-powerful, why doesn't He stop it? Or doesn't He have the power?"

Now, we live in a free world. We are not robots, with somebody feeding us information to do what he wants. We are not machines no matter how clever, who are operated by some heavenly intelligence. We are human beings, and this means we are free. Free to live or destroy. To love or hate. To fight or make peace. Obviously, we haven't been doing too well!

In our freedom we are allowed to create weapons of destruction. Man has always had such weapons, from primitive clubs and bows and arrows to the menacing nuclear arms of our time. Man is free. And he always manages to misuse that freedom. Why should we blame God for war?

If we invent cars, why accuse God of the carnage on the highways? If we are free to live as we please, why blame Him because some get drunk? Is God at fault when a drunk runs down my child? Man's freedom makes such evil possible. And we can't lay this at the doorstep of God.

"All right, I'll go along with that. Man is to blame for much of it. But I heard of a surgeon who expects to carry a cancer cell with him to the throne of God and

27

ask 'why?' What about mentally deficient children? How can a good God permit this?"

I told you before that we're chipping away at an iceberg, nine-tenths of which is below the surface. It won't go away. There are no adequate explanations. The parents of a child with the mentality of a four-year-old live with it every day. As the child grows up, they are reminded of their problem. And every day they have their choice again—to rebel against whatever gods there be, or to accept. Always that terrible choice. And that is the ultimate issue. Rebellion or acceptance?

A young and pure Christian girl was attacked and raped. In an honest letter to her pastor she asked how she could accept this terrible experience and still believe in a God of love. Her pastor wrote: "Perhaps that will be one of the *last* things we will be able to work out. Perhaps only at the day of judgment." Here we can only learn to walk by faith. Of course, he went on to say, that's a great deal to ask. But maybe it is man's supreme challenge—whether he walks by faith (and accepts) or by sight (and rebels).

You see, even to suggest that this is a trial brought into your life, is not enough of an explanation either. We do not really enjoy trials. We don't want to be tested by Somebody up there. We are not playthings. Neither would we keep on testing our children in this manner.

The old story of Job is all about suffering. Job lost his entire family, children and grandchildren, all his possessions and finally his health. If any man ever suffered, it was Job. But those who look on the story of Job simply as a test, fail to grasp the significance of it. For Job, suffering turned into an experience of the living God. And that experience gave value to his great trial.

Now, would you rather have Job's faith in spite of all his troubles, or Oscar Wilde's skepticism when he said that there's enough suffering in one street in London to prove that God does not love man? That's your choice. Would it be easier to explain suffering without a loving God? Would it be more comforting to believe in chance or fate or even a cruel, evil force at the helm of the universe? That would really send us into depression!

But now I must tell you where I think the Christian answer *really* lies. For this you must move beyond Job to Jesus. Jesus never submitted any theories about suffering. He was asked about it, of course, but He made no attempts to explain it away, to smooth it over, or to offer theological solutions. He did not say it was God's will, or a trial, nor that we should escape from it. To the contrary—He told us to take up our cross.

And He took up His. He suffered in our midst. And if He is God in human flesh (which you may not accept as yet) this would mean that *God* entered man's world of woe, even to the point of dying on a cross.

Now, you see, I've changed the question. I'm not asking *why* God allows suffering. I'm asking: Why did God suffer? You can see the difference yourself. Why did God allow His only Son to suffer? He could have stopped it. He was not powerless. But He didn't. Why?

Just as a good father will not do all his son's homework for him while he sends him out to play, so God, the Father, did not interfere. He did not stop the whole process of crucifixion, and more important still— God suffered as a Father for His only Son! (Do you know of any greater misery than losing your only son?) There is no suffering which God has not tasted. Willingly! This is the meaning of the cross. This is what took place there. And this means a whole new way of looking at suffering.

What does it mean? God, in love, did not remain aloof. He became involved in life, in death, in pain. If this is the God who has shown Himself to man, can we still charge Him with the enigmas we face in life? Somehow, it doesn't seem quite right.

"But you've not really answered the question. You've not explained it."

No, I haven't. You're right. I've not solved anything for you. But instead of asking why, now I'm asking *how*. How can I meet these tragedies? Not, *why* has it happened to me, but since it has happened, will I sink or swim?

And that means (at least for me) that the iceberg is melting. I may not be able to chip away at it with my small pick, but the sun has come out (God's sun), and that iceberg is actually fading away. A woman said after her husband's death: "I'm remembering my cup is half-full instead of half-empty." That can happen in the light of the cross.

Have you noticed something else? I've taken the accent away from suffering and placed it on love. You asked, "How can a loving God allow so much *suffering*?" Now I'm talking about this *loving* God.

"For God so loved the world, that he gave his only begotten Son, that whosoever believeth in him should not perish, but have everlasting life."[1] One little word is often overlooked in this famous verse. God *so* loved. This is how God loved. This is what He did. This is how—at the cross!

Without solving the problem I've said, "Look at the cross." Give it some thought. Consider Jesus' love and the love of the Father. If He did not interfere with the crime of all crimes, why should He suddenly stop your suffering? Or mine? God does not protect us when we pay our little installments of faith and prayer. We hold

30

no special insurance policy to escape suffering. The good are not immune. Jesus wasn't.

"But," you say, "others have died on crosses, and what of all the martyrs in history? What of those who were burned at stakes or torn to bits by wild beasts or gassed to death in concentration camps? What of those who must live with terrible problems? Why make so much of this one crucifixion of Jesus?"

Of course many have died as martyrs and suffered all kinds of torture. And many more must endure great trials in life. My emphasis is not on the type of death, but on the Person who died. The cross in itself does not make the suffering valuable. The One who suffered on that cross makes it meaningful.

You're really asking about Jesus. Who is Jesus? Why is *His* death so significant? Why focus all attention on that *one* cross? We will deal with this next time. For now, let me sum up:

To explain suffering as punishment is far too weak. Nor is it understood merely as the will of God. That's a part of it; but the only person who can make that acknowledgment is the one who experiences it from within. Suffering is more than a test. To Job it brought an experience of God.

The Christian points to the cross of Jesus. Only wounds can heal wounds. Analysis and explanation fall short. Jesus never explained. He suffered. So has God suffered too. Our misery has touched Him. Therefore He can heal and bind up our wounds, if we will believe. . . . We walk by faith and not by sight.

Life begins as a problem. That problem is tremendous, even tragic. But if it ends well, it ends in faith. It is a great problem and therefore we must have a great faith. Our main need is not to find an explanation but a victory. Isn't that your real concern? You don't want a

31

theory. You want power to face life. And here, if you will receive it, is where to look for the secret:

"To us, the greatest demonstration of God's love for us has been his sending his only Son into the world to give us life through him. We see real love, not in the fact that we loved God, but that he loved us and sent his Son to make personal atonement for our sins."[2]

Notes

[1]John 3:16, KJV   [2]I John 4:9,10

CHAPTER 5

Now, What about Jesus?

It's unavoidable. In these conversations we're going
to have to discuss Him, aren't we? For generally you
have a thousand questions about Jesus. You may begin
by asking: "How can you be sure that Jesus lived? You
Christians base everything on Jesus. How do you know
He was really here?"

Isn't it strange that this question should even come
up? Why are there people who ask whether Jesus lived,
who never at the same time question the existence of
Plato or Aristotle? Do you suppose that's because Christians affirm that He is the Son of God? Or that Jesus is
considered more than an ordinary man? Do you suppose
that's why people deny His very existence, because they
don't want to face the questions?

"I don't know," you say, "I myself think there was
such a person, but is there any mention of Him outside
of the Bible?"

33

Yes, there is. A Jewish historian named Josephus wrote a history of the Jews. He lived in the first century, and he mentioned Jesus briefly. Two Roman historians, Tacitus and Pliny the Younger, describing the persecution of Christians, also speak of Jesus. "The source of the name (Christians) was Christus, who in the principate of Tiberius had been put to death by the procurator Pontius Pilate," wrote Tacitus in A.D. 115.

But you realize, don't you, that your question raises a much bigger point! What of Christianity itself? What of the church? Could it have started apart from such a person? If there had been no Jesus, what a gigantic hoax was pulled by a handful of fishermen! That defies all reason.

"I'll go along. There had to be someone. OK. But why all this emphasis on Jesus? I suppose He was a good man, a simple man, a teacher, a prophet. But why more than that? Why make Him into the Son of God?"

Let's agree that He was a good man, and a great teacher. We don't have to say He was the greatest, but certainly one of the best. If we can also agree that He was a prophet, then here's my question: What did He have to say? What did He teach?

"That's easy," you say. "Love your neighbor. Live by the golden rule. Turn the other cheek. Believe in God. Be a good Samaritan. That about sums it up. Live a good life."

True. But if that's all He said, then let's not make so much fuss about Him. Then He is no different from other religious teachers. They may have put it differently, but Confucius taught the golden rule and Buddha certainly talked about the good life. And you can add a lot of other people to the list of prophets and teachers.

I think you'll have to look elsewhere to find out what produced Christianity. There was something else Jesus emphasized. And there was something else He did.

34

"Oh, you mean the miracles? Well, don't ask me to believe those farfetched stories. I'm tired of people telling me that I must believe the miracles. I can't, that's all."

How do you think He performed those miracles?

"I don't know. I don't really care. I don't believe in miracles. I don't see miracles today—but I'll listen to what you have to say."

Fair enough. And thanks for the opportunity. Perhaps you think of miracles as magic tricks. And why should Jesus lower Himself to become a magician? You may think it's beneath His dignity. But, of course, that's hardly the way to look at the miracles.

You'll agree that there are some laws and rules which man hasn't discovered yet. Modern science has discovered so much that we have the notion that this is all there is to it. But even the scientists will tell you it's only the beginning. Modern science, in fact, gives us quite a clue to these miracles.

Suppose a person can be greatly helped by talking to a psychiatrist. *Only* talking. No drugs, no medication, no shock treatments. Could we say, if this person is transformed, that a miracle took place in his thinking?

Or, consider the so-called miracle drugs. (Now there's a name for you!) If medication can put your system in balance or close off the worrying part of your mind, isn't that a miracle? Besides, do physicians clearly understand how people are healed? Talk to your doctor about that. They're not so sure. They're even foggy about the influence of the mind on the body. (Over half of the patients in our institutions, including hospitals, are there because of mental and not physical disorders.)

So I ask you: Could you admit the possibility that Jesus, without the use of drugs and keenly conscious of the power of God, can change people?

"All right," you say, "let us suppose that Jesus was

able to help people who had mental problems, and everybody considered these miracles. That doesn't explain the feeding of five thousand people with a couple of pieces of bread, or walking on the water, or bringing bodies back from the dead."

As I said, there are rules behind the rules we have discovered, of which we know nothing. The vast unknown. We're now transplanting hearts, taking the heart from a dead person and giving added life to the living. In a way that's raising something dead, isn't it? It was certainly unheard of prior to 1968. As to resurrection, the Bible asks this very logical question: "Why does it seem incredible to you all that God should raise the dead?"[1]

We don't know as much about walking on the water as we know about gravitation. Perhaps if we knew more, it wouldn't sound so incredible. But, how would flying through air have sounded to those who lived before the twentieth century? There is always the possibility that since we can now walk in space (and we know man is heavier than air), that one day we'll learn to walk on the water as well.

You see, the moment you admit the existence of *God*, you leave the door wide open. Take the feeding of the five thousand. It was not an attention-getting device. It was the necessity of the moment. And that's quite important, too. Jesus never performed miracles for miracle's sake. He met very human and very real needs.

Much of our skepticism toward miracles stems from a philosopher named David Hume. People aren't aware of this of course, but Hume said that if anything only happened once, it probably didn't happen. To prove something it should be repeatable, like a scientific experiment. By Hume's standards, therefore, the entry of God into the world (which is the biggest miracle of all) is not probable. It only happened once. Then all the miracles which resulted from the incarnation (God becoming man) are also improbable. How about the history of the world? It only happened once. Is it therefore not true? How about you as an individual? You only happened once! Are you or are you not unique? There is no one quite like you, you know.

I can't make you believe in the miracles, but I can suggest that you read the life of Jesus with this question in mind: "If I slice out all the miracles, what do I have left?" Augustine once wrote: "I should not be a Christian but for the miracles." And Blaise Pascal: "There would be no sin in disbelieving Jesus Christ if it were not for the miracles."

What if Jesus knew more than we do even now, about *God's* rules, that is? Isn't it possible, therefore, that He was able to perform what we now loosely term "miracles"? You are willing to give this some thought, I know. And that's all I ask you to do.

"All right, suppose Jesus lived and taught the golden rule. Perhaps He performed some miracles. Others have performed miracles. In the Old Testament for example, Moses and the prophets. Other religions have all sorts of miracle stories too. What makes Jesus so different then? Surely not only miracles?"

Good question. We've talked about miracles a bit because it came up in our conversation. But it's not the unique thing. I really expected to take you down a different road. Let's take it now.

I asked you earlier what Jesus taught and you replied: "The golden rule, love your neighbor, believe in God, do good, and so on." That's not very distinctive! What else did He say? What did He say about Himself? Did He consider Himself simply a teacher who pointed others to the truth?

You see, I find in the words of Jesus something very distinctive. I'll put it like this. Instead of pointing away

37

from Himself, saying, "That is the truth, over there; follow it," Jesus pointed to Himself and said: "I myself am the truth. Follow me."[2]

"But if I remember anything at all from the words of Jesus, it's simply that He called Himself the Son of Man. He was very humble. He didn't refer to Himself as the Son of God."

Yes, He called Himself the Son of Man. That has a very human sound to it. Jesus called Himself fully and completely man. "Son of Man" means representative man, man as man ought to be.

But "Son of Man" is also a title, a title for the Messiah. It held this meaning for the Jews. They considered the Messiah as the Saviour who would free Israel. By saying that He was the Son of Man, Jesus declared Himself the Saviour of Israel. Son of Man and Son of God are not opposites, as you might suppose.

"But did He ever call Himself the Son of God? Or is this what the disciples said about Him?"

Let's consider only the words of Jesus. Take this passage for example: "The dead will hear the voice of the Son of God and when they have heard it they will live!" Here Jesus not only calls Himself the Son of God, He also proclaims His ability to raise the dead.

He continues: "For just as the Father has life in himself, so by the Father's gift the Son also has life in himself." He holds the ability to give life. And because He is both Son of God *and* Son of Man, He has authority to judge: "And he has given him authority to judge because he is Son of Man."[3]

Or again: "I and the Father are one," said Jesus. The Jews reacted violently. They were ready to kill Him: "You, who are only a man, are making yourself out to be God," they charged. Then He replied: "I said, 'I am the Son of God.' If I fail to do what my Father does, then do not believe me. But if I do, even though you have no faith in me personally, then believe in the things that I do. Then you may come to know and realize that the Father is in me and I am in the Father."[4]

"You have only been quoting from the Gospel of John. What about the other gospels? Do any of them report this?"

"Nobody knows the Son except the Father. Nor does anyone know the Father except the Son—and the man to whom the Son chooses to reveal him."[5] That is certainly clear.

The great confession by Peter is in Matthew, Mark and Luke. After Jesus asked them whom they thought He was, Peter replied: "You are Christ, the Son of the living God."[6]

True. Jesus did not say it. Peter said it. But if Peter were wrong, wouldn't Jesus have corrected him at once? He did, in fact, correct Peter a moment later when Peter opposed Him on another matter.[7] Therefore it follows that if Peter had been wrong in calling Jesus the Son of God, Jesus would not have hesitated to set him straight.

Instead He seemed overjoyed: "Simon, son of Jonah, you are a fortunate man indeed! . . . it was not your own nature but my Heavenly Father who has revealed this truth to you!"[8]

Read the life of Jesus for yourself. Make up your own mind. This is the way He would want it. You see, never once did Jesus *force* belief on His disciples. He allowed them to discover it for themselves. The episode I have quoted just now took place after Jesus had been with them for two years. During that time He did not indoctrinate them. It was revealed from above, and He encouraged them in their faith.

"I still find it difficult to believe all this. After all, those gospels were written by men. They were also written much later after Jesus lived. How can we be sure of them then? How can we trust them? People passed on these stories and they got juicier as they went along. So this may have all been added. . . ."

We'll have to take up the question of the authenticity of the Bible next. Of course it's vital for accepting the gospel stories. But now let's see where we've been.

Jesus was a good man. He was a great teacher. If we accept Him as a teacher, we need to listen to what He taught. A man who said about Himself what Jesus said, would be either a quack, a madman, deceived and a deceiver, the devil himself—or God. You must make up your mind about that. But don't keep on saying merely that He was a good man and a great teacher. That's *not* one of the choices.

" 'The difference between us,' Jesus said to them, 'is that you come from below and I am from above. You belong to this world but I do not. . . . He who sent me is true, and I am only speaking to this world what I myself have heard from him.' "[9]

I believe Jesus is the Son of God because He said so. All the other evidence of His life, His teaching, His works convince me. It is the only logical conclusion, once you're willing to take Him at face value. Did you know that the great author, Dostoevsky, who drew deeply on the life and person of Christ, once wrote: "I say that not only is there no one else like Jesus, but there could be no one. I would even say more. If anyone could prove to me that Christ is outside the truth, and if the truth did exclude Christ, I should prefer to stay with Christ and not with truth. . . ."

Notes

[1] Acts 26:8
[2] See John 14:6
[3] John 5:25–27
[4] John 10:30,33,36–38
[5] Matthew 11:27
[6] Matthew 16:16
[7] Matthew 16:21–23
[8] Matthew 16:17
[9] John 8:23,26

CHAPTER 6

But Can You Believe the Bible?

"It seems to me you Christians are always quoting the Bible. You base everything on the Bible. You want me to swallow a book. Well, I can't. The Bible is a good book, but it's old. It tells the history of the Jewish people, way back there. What good is that for me today? What can I gain from reading all those begats and begots? Who cares? Besides, the Bible is unscientific. It talks about the earth being flat. How can I accept that today? How can I believe in miracles? And if I can't believe in the Bible, I suppose I can't be a good Christian."

Now, hold on a moment! You've raised a lot of questions, and I don't know whether I can clear up some of this. But I think that your basic question which under-

41

lies all the others is simply: How can I accept that old book in modern times? How can I believe the Bible to be reliable and authentic?

Now let me approach this with something Jesus said: "Just as life went on in the days of Noah so will it be at the coming of the Son of Man. In those days before the flood people were eating, drinking, marrying and being given in marriage until the very day that Noah went into the ark, and . . . the flood . . . came and destroyed them all."[1]

Preachers usually have a field day with this passage. They talk about the sinful times before the flood. They turn to Genesis (where the flood is recorded) and show how wicked those people were. Therefore, they say, the flood came as a judgment from God. The last days will be full of crime, corruption, delinquency, sexual deviation, rebellion, and there you have the modern problems of man.

Actually, Jesus never brought up all that evil! He simply said they were eating and drinking and giving in marriage. Now, what's wrong with that? Nothing! (Christians eat and drink and marry.) What Jesus meant was that this was *all* they thought about. Eating, drinking, marrying, the world of business and pleasure —the secular environment—scientific, materialistic; and don't bother about God. Don't raise ultimate questions. Why not? Because they're not answerable. And if you can't answer them, you just don't raise them.

Here is the world's approach to life. And in that businesslike atmosphere does a book about God have any chance? It comes at you with God, and even, as the book itself says, *from* God. But if you have pretty well eliminated God from your thinking, if you're just busy making a living and having a good time, then the Bible sounds foreign indeed.

Perhaps that's our problem. Not that the Bible is out

of tune with the times, but that we are out of tune with eternity—with the real issues!

"Yes, but wait a minute," you say. "The Bible is unscientific. How then can it speak to our scientific age? For example it says that the earth is flat. We know better. So, how can we accept the Bible at all?"

Where does it say that the earth is flat?

"Well, I, eh—I don't know exactly where, but it speaks about the four corners of the earth—somewhere."

Couldn't that be figurative rather than literal? Does 'corner' have to be taken in a literal sense? "At what time did the sun rise this morning?" Oh, I shouldn't have said that, should I? The sun doesn't rise. I ought to ask: "At what moment did the earth rotate into the position where the sun became visible this morning?" But who puts it that way, even in our scientific age?

OK. Forget that argument. I didn't mean to be flip about it. How can we expect a people to have the knowledge of Galileo or Copernicus, when they lived more than a thousand years before them? Though they were inspired by God in the writing of the Bible, they were not given scientific information in advance of their times. Would it not have sounded ridiculous for Ezekiel to announce the theory of relativity in his visions?

Not only ridiculous, but *unnecessary!* The Bible aims in a different direction. Inspiration is not a matter of giving scientific enlightenment. "All scripture is inspired by God and is useful for teaching the faith and correcting error, for resetting the direction of a man's life and training him in good living."[2] This is the purpose of Scripture.

On the other hand, take the emerging science of psychology. It could very well be built on the insights of the Bible. A professor of psychiatry stated to a minister (Ian Burnett): "Within the Bible there is far more wis-

43

dom and insight and help and guidance and truth concerning ourselves and the way of true abundant life than there is in all the books of psychology put together." Quite a statement.

Or consider another psychiatrist, Dr. James T. Fisher: "If you were to take the sum total of all the authoritative articles ever written by the most qualified of psychologists and psychiatrists and refine them and cleave out the excess verbiage . . . you would have an awkward and incomplete summation of the Sermon on the Mount."

"But what about all those begats? It's dull stuff. Why do I have to plow through all that history? What good is it? Some people are interested in history, but I'm not."

Well, if you'll read the Old Testament, you have my permission to skip over those genealogies. The reason why they're there is to show the continuity of Israel—their relationship to Abraham and the fathers. That creates solidarity. We still have people who are interested in their family trees. Most Americans trace their ancestry to some foreign country.

But don't think the Old Testament is all history. It isn't. There are psalms of praise and proverbs of wisdom, prophetic insights and ethical teachings. And the purpose of the Old Testament is to prepare for the Messiah, the Saviour of the world. He was to come through His people, Israel. And through this great story God reveals His dealings with man.

You now bring up another point: "There are contradictions in the Bible. How can I believe the Bible if it is full of contradictions?"

I know before you even mention it what you're going to say. You're going to ask how an eye for an eye and a tooth for a tooth can be reconciled with turning the other cheek. That's a contradiction, isn't it?

44

"Yes, that's one. Of course there are others. But that one does bother me. So what am I supposed to do? Pretend it isn't there?"

You can't ignore it. The only way to examine a contradiction such as this is to consider the context. Who said it? Why did he say it? For what purpose was it said? And so on.

Now "an eye for an eye and a tooth for a tooth" came from Moses. It followed the giving of the Ten Commandments.[3] Moses was setting down laws for the nation. Such rules were established that the people might be governed in justice. This was a judicial system of order and law.

In the Sermon on the Mount Jesus quoted the law and ventured beyond it toward an individualistic ethic: "You have heard that it used to be said '*An eye for an eye and a tooth for a tooth*,' but I tell you, don't resist the man who wants to harm you. If a man hits your right cheek, turn the other one to him as well."[4]

Jesus did not establish this as a law for the courts. Jesus was speaking to His disciples. His was an ethic for the individual, not for the entire judicial system of the world. Christians are not to seek revenge. They are to live in forgiveness and peace. If you apply Jesus' words to legal matters, you miss the point. Should the entire judicial system turn the other cheek to criminals? A Christian may decide to go to court if someone takes advantage of him. He'll have to find out what God wants him to do in such a matter.

So, you see, seeming contradictions will disappear under closer scrutiny. Each passage must be considered in its context.

"But my basic question still remains," you say. "How can I believe in the Bible? How can I accept the words of Jesus? The Bible was written hundreds of years later. It was all passed on from generation to genera-

45

tion and they kept adding to it. So, how can we actually know what Jesus said?"

The Bible was, of course, written after the actual events, but not hundreds of years after. That bothers a lot of people. It bothered me too. I had many questions about this when I went to seminary. I had heard that John had not written the Gospel of John, and Paul had not written most of the letters which bore his name.

When I arrived at Princeton Seminary, I made a thorough study of this and listened carefully to what the professors taught. If I were to condense those years of study for you, I would say that most twentieth century scholars who are aware of the manuscript evidence declare that the entire New Testament was written before A.D. 100. This means that since the crucifixion took place around A.D. 30, the New Testament was written in one generation.

There is a fragment from the Gospel of John (chapter 18, recounting the trial of Jesus before Pilate) in the John Rylands Library in Manchester, England. This is a very remarkable fragment, for it was found in Egypt in a small town along the Nile. It had originally been written by John in Ephesus, probably around A.D. 90. Now twenty years later, it turns up translated into a different language, in Egypt. Some scholars date the fragment around A.D. 110-120. Visible proof in Manchester that the *last* of the gospels was written before A.D. 100.

Actually, most of the New Testament was completed before A.D. 70. Let's do a little detective work to figure this out for ourselves.

Fact 1: The Gospel according to Luke is addressed to a man named Theophilus.[5]

Fact 2: The book of Acts is addressed to a man named Theophilus.[6]

Conclusion: In all probability Luke wrote both the

46

Gospel and the book of Acts. (There are of course many other factors which point to Luke as the author of both books.)

Fact 3: The central figure which dominates the book of Acts (chapter 9 to the end) is the apostle Paul. We read of his conversion, his missionary travels and his trip to Rome. Since we know that he died in Rome, we'd expect the book of Acts to end with Paul's death. It would be the obvious climax. But it *doesn't.* Acts concludes with Paul still in Rome, where he "gave them the teaching of the Lord Jesus Christ."[7]

Conclusion: This book was written *before* the death of Paul. It had to be. Luke finished it without a proper conclusion. When did Paul die? Historians generally place his death around A.D. 65-67.

Fact 4: That means the book of Acts was written by A.D. 65.

Fact 5: Since the Gospel according to Luke and the Acts were written by the same man, the Gospel probably antedated the early church history by a few years.

Fact 6: In his introduction Luke tells us that he considered many other sources. The experts put Mark's Gospel among these which Luke examined. That pushes the Gospel of Mark to a very early time; some scholars place it between A.D. 40 and 50.

Do you see how close to the times of Jesus the New Testament actually comes? It was written by eyewitnesses: "We actually saw his majesty with our own eyes. . . . We actually heard that voice speaking from Heaven while we were with him on the sacred mountain." "It was *life* which appeared before us: we saw it, we are eyewitnesses of it, and are now writing to you about it."[8]

You can believe the Bible to be authentic. I hope you have noticed that I am not merely giving you my personal ideas, but *facts.*

47

"I still say that the writers may have embellished it. They tried hard to make a case for the divinity of Jesus. How can I be sure they didn't?"

You are now questioning their honesty, aren't you? But that's all right. Here's a statement that convinces me of their reliability. Jesus was speaking of the coming of the Kingdom of God and the judgment: "But about that actual day and time no one knows—not even the angels of Heaven, nor the Son, only the Father."[9]

Now, if they were trying so desperately to establish Jesus as the Son of God, why include Jesus' ignorance? If you had been Matthew, building a case, wouldn't the inclusion of that saying do damage to it? (It shows the limitations of Jesus as a man.) Wouldn't you just as soon have dropped it? Scratched it? But Matthew did not leave it out.

Look. The Bible's all right. And if you'll read it with an open mind, you'll find that out. Go ahead and ask questions. But consider the evidence.

The Bible is a little like a road map. I suppose taking a vacation trip is more exciting than looking at a map. The scenery of god's creation is far better than a piece of colored paper. But remember that without that piece of paper, you'll probably get lost. Of course if you want to get lost, throw the map away. But if you don't, it might just turn out to be the way to an experience of the living God.

Notes

[1]Matthew 24:37–39
[2]II Timothy 3:16
[3]Exodus 21:23–25
[4]Matthew 5:38,39
[5]Luke 1:3

[6]Acts 1:1
[7]Acts 28:31
[8]II Peter 1:16,17; I John 1:2
[9]Matthew 24:36

CHAPTER 7

How It All Began

Would it surprise you to know that the first Christians didn't have a Bible? They had the Old Testament, to be sure, but they didn't have a New Testament until it was written.

We generally think that the Bible produced the church. That's not true. The church produced the Bible. The early Christians went preaching everywhere without a Bible under their arm.

"But most Christians always go back to the Bible. They are always telling me to believe in the Bible, to read the Bible. All they quote is the Bible. It's all you ever hear."

I know what you mean. That's why I'm raising this point. What is the Bible?

"Christians say that it's the Word of God."

I thought that's what you'd say. In a sense the Bible *is* the Word of God. It tells about God. It was inspired by God, written through His chosen prophets and apostles. But the Bible is more than the Word of God. It is the record of an event. It tells about this event. It bears witness to this event. And what is of supreme importance, in the last analysis, is not the *record* but the event itself!

As I said a moment ago, these early Christians didn't have a Bible under their arm when they went out into the world to preach. But they started a movement which has spread throughout the whole earth. They did it without Bibles, without buildings, without budgets, without the institutional church.

The Bible, then, arose out of the life of the church; that is, from the early Christians. The New Testament was written to tell the story of Jesus to those who came after the apostles. The next generation needed a record in their hands of what God had done through Jesus of Nazareth. So they wrote about it.

The New Testament letters of Paul, Peter, James and others were written to people after they had become Christians. These letters explained Christianity, instructed them in the faith, answered some of their questions and helped them through their problems. This is how the New Testament grew out of the church.

"But what did these first Christians preach? And how did they preach without the Bible, without quotations? All some people do today is quote the Bible."

Exactly. You're beginning to see my point. They preached without being able to quote such and such a book, chapter and verse. Christianity, therefore, came into being not because of a book—even though it is the Bible—but because of an event. Something had happened. The apostles were witnesses of it. That's how it all began. The event is what Christianity is all about.

"What are you talking about?" you ask. "An event. *What* event? If they didn't have a Bible, what did they tell people to believe in? I don't get it."

Isn't it hard for us to understand this? We have been so conditioned the other way. But when you see it *this* way, you will realize that Christians are not asking you to swallow a book. No, you don't have to swallow that book! Can you imagine Peter standing up before a group of Jews, saying: "You have to swallow a book. A new book. You believe in the Old Testament. Here is the New Testament. Accept it. Become Christians. It is the Word of God."

Nothing of the sort! When he stood up, he spoke about Jesus. You want to know what they preached? Here it is in capsule form. A Roman officer had sent for the apostle Peter. He wanted to become a Christian. This is what Peter said to him:

God "has sent His message to the sons of Israel by giving us the good news of peace through Jesus Christ —he is the Lord of us all. You must know the story of Jesus of Nazareth—why, it has spread through the whole of Judaea, beginning from Galilee after the baptism that John proclaimed. You must have heard how God anointed him with the power of the Holy Spirit, of how he went about doing good and healing all who suffered from the devil's power—because God was with him. Now we are eyewitnesses of everything that he did, both in the Judaean country and in Jerusalem itself, and yet they murdered him by hanging him on a cross. But on the third day God raised that same Jesus and let him be clearly seen, not indeed by the whole people, but by witnesses whom God had previously chosen. We are those witnesses, we who ate and drank with him after he had risen from the dead! . . . It is to him that all the prophets bear witness, that every man

51

who believes in him may receive forgiveness of sins through his name."[1]

Nothing about a book! The book records what happened when God became man. It is the record of that event. But the event is what the apostles called the good news.

That's the issue you have to face. Not merely to believe the Bible. The proclamation which changed the world was that in Jesus of of Nazareth, God has actually visited our planet. He has come in person. The demonstration is in the life, the acts, and ultimately the death and resurrection of Jesus. "God was in Christ personally reconciling the world to himself."[2] That's the incredible good news.

Consider your alternative. Suppose you can't accept it. Then, whatever "God" you believe in remains an overwhelming "Power," an infinite "Mind," a huge "Unknown"—in short, a distant, impersonal and disinterested God, intelligent, but unconcerned about man —almighty perhaps, but not necessarily loving.

The Christian message proclaims that God is focused in a person, a person who acts surprisingly like Him! God makes Himself known to man, not by shouting orders at us from "Up There," or writing commandments across the sky. Not even by choosing a prophet. No, God becomes flesh and assures us of His concern. Now we *know* that God is love. Love always acts, communicates. Love is something you do. Love is something God has done.

That's what they preached about. That event. The love of God led Him not only to enter the world. It also took Him to a cross. And that's hard to understand. If this is God in human flesh, why did He let Himself get killed? Did that make any sense whatsoever? To us this is the supreme expression of the love of God. Christians explain that He did it in love. His

52

sacrifice was for our sins. He suffered in our place, and with His stripes we are healed.

But that wasn't all. God raised Jesus from the dead. The apostles bore witness to this crucial event in the history of the world. Who else has ever come back from the dead? The apostles proclaimed the incarnation, the crucifixion and the resurrection—"Jesus is Lord of us all."

"Now you're preaching at me."

I don't mean to preach.

"I can't believe in the crucifixion. What good does it do me that Jesus died? What was the point of it? And the resurrection is more than I can accept at this moment. People don't come back from the dead. Maybe it was a spiritual thing. I don't know. Anyway, *that* is the event you're talking about—right?"

Right. That's how it all began. We'll have to spend some time discussing both the crucifixion and the resurrection later. I've only brought it up now since it was integral to the preaching of the early Christians. And they did it, remember, without the benefit of a written text, without the Bible.

Consider the note of authenticity: "We are eyewitnesses of everything that he did, both in the Judaean country and in Jerusalem itself. . . . We are those witnesses, we who ate and drank with him after he had risen from the dead." They did not try to *prove* the resurrection. They only said they were witnesses of the event.

What is a witness? He is a person who relates what he has seen and heard. In court he takes the stand and answers questions. If he did not see anything, if he doesn't know anything, he is dismissed. But he has a right to state what he has observed.

The early Christians identified themselves as witnesses. Nothing more. They simply conveyed their story: "We are the men whom he commanded to preach to the people and bear fearless witness to the fact that he is the one appointed by God to be the judge of both the living and the dead."[3]

He who died and rose again is Judge of all. Can you grasp this? You generally think of God as Judge. They announced Jesus as Judge of the world.

But He is also the Saviour. All who believe in Him will be forgiven. He accepts them and gives them eternal life. This is the good news. And those who believe are changed.

Not everybody believed it, of course. When Paul came to Athens he experienced mixed reactions. Some laughed at him. Others said they'd listen some other time, and a few believed.[4] By the way, the preaching of Paul was along the same lines as that of Peter. We have been looking at a model sermon from the early Christian community. There are several such sermons in the book of Acts, and they all relate this great event which brought the church into being.

"And that's how it all began? The Bible came later?"

Yes. But I must add one other factor. I know even before I mention this that you will raise your eyebrows and look at me quizzically. It will sound to you as if I'm a magician, about to pull a dove out of a hat.

What I'm talking about is the Holy Spirit. (The fact is that the Bible sometimes uses the dove as a symbol for the Holy Spirit!) You see, this biblical account of Peter talking to the Roman officer closes with these words: "While Peter was still speaking these words the Holy Spirit fell upon all who were listening to his message. The Jewish believers who had come with Peter were absolutely amazed that the gift of the Holy Spirit was being poured out on Gentiles also; for they heard them speaking in foreign tongues and glorifying God."[5]

This means that the Spirit of God worked in and

54

through those early Christians, just as we believe He is working in and through the church today. This is God's Spirit with man. The living God—present, actual, real.

I'm sure we'll have to discuss this "Holy Spirit" later on. All I want to say at this time is that these Christians lived *differently*. Not through sheer will power. Not through human effort. That's not possible. It doesn't work. But by some greater power within. We call Him the Holy Spirit.

The point I'm driving at is that this Spirit was present, leading men to joyously affirm that great event. He worked through the apostles producing the church, and later the Holy Scriptures.

"It's beginning to sound more and more like magic. The Holy Spirit? What am I supposed to believe? Instead of getting closer, I sometimes think I'm getting farther and farther away the more we talk."

Yes, I know. I've had that same experience myself. So, let me simplify it. You have a choice. Concentrate on money, sex, status, good looks and good times. Keep the radio on. Move in the crowd. Dope yourself up and read only the papers. Or—take one sentence from the teaching of Jesus and put it to the test.

"If anyone wants to do God's will," said Jesus, "he will know whether my teaching is from God or whether I merely speak on my own authority."[6] If you really want to know, then this is the way to go. Do God's will. Not in an academic way, but in actual practice. *Do* something. (Love is something you do.) Put His teaching into practice. Experience is the way to truth.

I'm not leaving you much room to argue about this. I'm aware of that. It's really a little infuriating. So, instead of arguing, why not take Jesus at His word? What do you have to lose? You may even discover something. . . .

Can you possibly remember when you first learned

55

how to multiply and divide, or struggled with fractions and algebra? For a while all seemed like mystery. Then, suddenly, something clicked. You saw the whole thing. You were no longer on the outside. You were "in the know."

Now, what happened? Nine chances out of ten you can't even recall. (I know it always happened to me without too much trouble, until I came to calculus. Then nothing happened!)

Something like this takes place in people when they first become Christians. You can never quite put your finger on it. You're not supposed to. All you know is that suddenly you're no longer on the outside trying to understand Christianity. You're on the inside—you've been given understanding.

That's about all I can say. Be open. Experiment. Follow through in action. Who knows? The scales may fall from your eyes and you will suddenly see. Jesus said something very interesting about that:

"The Spirit of the Lord is upon me,
Because he anointed me to preach good tidings to
    the poor. . . .
And recovering of sight to the blind."[7]

Notes

[1]Acts 10:36–43
[2]II Corinthians 5:19
[3]Acts 10:41,42
[4]Acts 17:30–34

[5]Acts 10:44,45
[6]John 7:17
[7]Luke 4:18

CHAPTER 8

Isn't Religion Just a Crutch?

Remember the time we had lunch together? We settled down in our booth and gave our order to the waitress, and then you came out with it.

"Look," you said, "We've had several talks about Christianity, and now I want you to level with me. No pretenses. Straight from the shoulder. Is it really true? Have you been honest with me about all this? Do you really believe it yourself? You're a minister and as a minister you have to keep up a front. Well, you don't have to do that with me. Be honest. I'm asking you straight out. Is it really true, or is Christianity just make-believe?"

You know, it's really impossible to convince someone else of your honesty. It's something you have to take on faith, just like marriage ought to begin in mutual trust. You'll have to take my word for it. If you really knew me, as you're beginning to through these conversations, you'd know that I couldn't live with myself if I had to play a game of make-believe.

Perhaps some people can. Some do. They don't give it too much thought. They just accept. They believe. When an authority figure says something, they follow like sheep.

"That's what I mean," you said. "People just swallow it. Never give it any thought. But, then, you're not like that. So I want to know it from you. Is it real? Or is religion just a crutch?"

Do you realize that the very fact you're asking these questions means that you haven't written Christianity off as nonsense? You've not discarded it, or else you wouldn't be pressing me so hard.

But let me make a correction. People generally suppose that when the church says something, everybody automatically believes it. Or at least they're supposed to. But that is only true for the authoritarian churches. There are some of these; however the Reformation created a change. It put the Bible into people's hands. Why? So the church could control them? To the contrary. So people could think for themselves!

"But how many actually do?"

That's a good question. Most people pass through a rebellious stage, sometimes in their teens or twenties, sometimes later—even in their forties, which indicates that at some time we have to start thinking for ourselves. We can't accept other people's faith. We want to know.

"But that's exactly when people leave the church, when they begin to think for themselves. They drift away. They can't accept it any longer. That's what happened to me. I had some religion in my past, but

I've grown up now. I think for myself. I don't want a crutch. I don't want religion as a crutch."

We were served now, and as you bit into your sandwich I asked you whether you thought that religion is mostly for small children and old ladies.

"Well, when I walk into church, I see mostly older people. Not too many young ones. Teenagers drift away. Few are in their twenties and thirties. Where is everybody? Sometimes I think it is all for old ladies and kids in Sunday School. And I think these people use religion as a crutch."

You keep bringing up this crutch to me. Now, I would never be satisfied to think of Christianity as a crutch. I rebel against the whole idea. And if I thought for a moment that Christianity was supporting me like a crutch, I'd get rid of it and walk on my own two feet.

Nor do I consider the church to be only for old ladies and kids. You can't escape the fact that good-thinking men, brilliant men, men from all walks of life have given their allegiance to Jesus Christ. Presidents, statesmen, scientists, educators, philosophers and theologians. I don't want to quote you names, because then I'd sound like a TV commercial. You know, if such and such a movie star or football player smokes stinkies, then they ought to be great for the rank and file, too. That may be good sales psychology, but it's actually downgrading. Why are you less important than some movie star? Besides, I don't think Jesus needs the endorsement of a brilliant or famous person.

But let me face your challenge. A crutch, you say. Sometime ago a friend showed me a painting he had done. He's a good artist. This painting expressed his views.

A big man walked steadily down a road. He had a goal, a purpose. Behind him came a little man, a terribly small, ridiculous-looking little man. The little sim-

59

pleton was attempting to walk the same road as the big man. He was imitating. Furthermore, a chain connected him to the leader, and he was enslaved. He was not free. He was not an individual. And my friend called his painting: The Follower.

Isn't that the way you identify Christians? As weaklings? Unable to walk down their own road? Little followers? Why aren't we men enough to break the chains and become pathmakers ourselves?

Now, of course, this leads us smack into a problem. Jesus called fishermen, tax gatherers and others to join Him. "Follow Me," He said. Was this for the feeble only? For those who could not stand on their own two feet? There have always been such. And they have followed in His steps also. But Jesus intended something more.

For one thing He did not invite them to walk behind Him. He invited them to walk with Him. "I shall not call you servants any longer, for a servant does not share his master's confidence. No, I call you friends, now, because I have told you everything that I have heard from the Father."[1]

A friend does not follow in the rear. Nor is he bound by a chain. He is an equal and he is *free!* Consider also that the early disciples gave their lives for Jesus. They were men of conviction, men of vision, men of faith. And they marched straight into death. They were not hobbling on crutches. And what of the martyrs who followed them throughout the years?

Here's a description of Old Testament heroes which also applies to Christians: "Through their faith these men conquered kingdoms, ruled in justice and proved the truth of God's promises. They shut the mouths of lions, they quenched the furious blaze of fire, they escaped from death itself. From being weaklings they became strong men and mighty warriors . . . others were tortured and refused to be ransomed. . . . Others were exposed to the test of public mockery and flogging, and to the torture of being left bound in prison."[2]

Hardly crutches.

"All right," you said, as we both were talking more than we were eating, "What about prayer? Christians pray."

Not only Christians.

"But why do people pray? Isn't that a crutch? Isn't that an escape? Isn't it perhaps self-hypnosis?"

Well if it is self-hypnosis, why has prayer persisted all these years? Why should people continue to pray, if prayer never accomplishes anything?

"But I've tried prayer and it doesn't work! Nothing happens. You can't just say to a person with a problem: Pray, something will happen. I don't believe it. That's magic. That's crazy. It doesn't make sense."

I understand. And you're right in a way. But what do you mean you've *tried* prayer? Is it something to be tried like hypnosis or a two-week crash diet? Can you *use* prayer? Use it as you would manipulate another person to get a favor, or as you would give money under the table to vault you into higher places? Obviously when I put it like this you can see that prayer can't be tried or used.

What is prayer? Let me answer it this way. A child knows when his father isn't playing tricks on him, even though he may refuse to give him something. He may not understand why, but he learns to trust his father. Why? Because there's a relationship. And with that relationship comes communication. That's what prayer is —communication.

You pick up a telephone. But if there's no one on the other end, it's a cinch you won't keep on talking. You don't want to hold a monologue over the phone.

So how do you think of prayer? Do you expect any

answer? Have you ever thought about it as communication? And then, what do you expect?

"Well, that's a good question," you said. "I don't really know. But I still think it's for people who can't stand on their own two feet, or fight their own battles. They need help. So they pray. They're leaning on a crutch. In fact, there's a song called, 'Leaning on the Everlasting Arms.' That's the idea. It's all the same."

I know a man who was a real toughy. He made his own way in life. Nobody could tell him anything. And nobody tried. Dick, as we'll call him, was rough. Real rough. Prayer? He'd laugh at you if you'd mention it. That was for sissies.

Then Dick came up against some problems. He couldn't handle them. It may have started with his wife, his kids, his work, his parents and life in general, but a compulsion got the better of him. He had to drink and gamble. You can analyze that, explain it away, try to rationalize why he went that route, but the brutal fact is that he lost everything: his wife, his family, his home. Everything. Drank it all up and gambled it all away.

But Dick found what he called a higher Power. And he came back. Even now he's lost his wife and home, but he is holding his job. And he's not drinking or gambling. He's on the way. And this is what he says: "I didn't believe in prayer. I used to think with my emotions. When something came up, I used to go: This is it, I said. But now I listen. It's been dawning on me that something is working. It's become a challenge with me. I can't explain it. I know things are happening that are good. Prayer kind of enables me to see where I'm going and where I've been. It helps me to think clear."

Now call that a crutch if you want. I suggest that for Dick *alcohol* was the crutch and prayer has become a vital force, which is helping him get straightened out.

"Well, maybe it was his guilt that led him to pray. Maybe it's because people feel guilty that they think they have to lean on God. Is that what Christianity is for? To remove guilt?"

You were asking me some tough questions during our lunch. We had another cup of coffee. You were certainly getting to the heart of things.

There's no question about it, you see, that guilt will drive people to prayer. Every one of us has a handicap. Everyone has something to overcome. Fear. A habit. Anxiety. Temper. Resentment. Guilt.

Now you can ignore it, but it does no good. It just makes the problem bigger. Like cancer. It finally kills you.

Or you can try to handle it on your own. That sounds big. Someone once told me that he had overcome his drinking by sheer will power. He didn't need any help. He was back at it not long after. What if will power fails you?

Or you can ask for help. Whom would you bet on—a man who had a problem and refused to pray, or a man who had a problem and prayed?

Neither? OK. You got out of that one. How about this choice: A person who feels guilty, or a person who believes his guilt is definitely removed and is infinitely grateful?

Of course you'd rather be free from guilt. Who wouldn't? Then, this is the problem we ought to face. How do I get rid of guilt? How can I be free?

Jesus says: "You will know the truth and the truth will set you free!"[3] You've heard that before. But this is what He is actually talking about: "Believe me when I tell you that every man who commits sin is a slave. For a slave is no permanent part of a household, but a son is. If the Son, then, sets you free, you are really free."[4]

63

He gives us the assurance that he can set us free. It's not a crutch. It's the language of release, or emancipation, or freedom.

Look. Jesus tells about a man who goes into the temple to pray. He feels guilty, ashamed, unworthy. He stands there in the back and doesn't dare to approach God. All he can mutter is: "God, have mercy on a sinner like me."[5] That's all. That's his prayer. Not much of a prayer, is it?

He has expressed his faith in God. He hopes that he will be heard. He has no credentials. He asks no favors except mercy. And, according to Jesus, something did happen. He left the temple a different man. He experienced forgiveness. He had humbled himself, and God is merciful to the humble.

How did the help come? I don't know. But the fact is that like Dick, he became a different person. No matter how coldly or analytically you may rationalize prayer, you could never take that away from him. It was a true experience.

That's why I never look at Christianity as a crutch, when, after all, it's the only thing in the world that can set me *free!*

Notes

[1]John 15:15
[2]Hebrews 11:33–36
[3]John 8:32

[4]John 8:34–36
[5]Luke 18:13

CHAPTER 9

Pie in the Sky!

That day when we were having lunch together you were certainly full of questions. You wanted some down-to-earth answers, and we must have sat there for a couple of hours. It was a good thing no one wanted our booth, but we kept on drinking coffee anyway, so we wouldn't feel guilty about occupying the premises. After we'd discussed prayer and guilt, you leveled with me again.

"Look," you said, "don't most Christians stay with it because of the rewards they're going to get? Isn't that why the church hangs out rewards in heaven? And if you don't stay with it, you won't get there? Right? So they're afraid. They go for this pie-in-the-sky-by-and-by bit and toe the line. But isn't it all just like dangling a carrot in front of a donkey? Isn't that why people become Christians? To make it into heaven?"

No, I don't agree with you. Of course there may be those, but you'll agree it's not much of a motive. Besides, the church isn't offering a pot of gold at the end of the rainbow which isn't there. You can't tell people about heaven if you don't believe in it yourself.

"That's what I mean," you said. "Do *you* believe in heaven?"

Look. Anyone who still thinks the sky's the limit has no imagination. Can you conceive of a God who would create all this and end it with the grave? What would be the point of creating life and then chopping it off? Even the ancient cultures believed in the continuity of life—crude beliefs to be sure, but immortality nevertheless.

Socrates told his friends that "no evil can happen to a good man, either in life or in death." And Spinoza, that great Jewish philosopher, concluded that the human mind cannot be absolutely destroyed. Something remains which is eternal.

"But isn't it possible to believe in God without believing in heaven?"

How? If you believe in God, you believe in eternity. God is the Eternal. He is not bound to time. Therefore how can you fancy a God without eternity, without heaven?

We are almost completely earthbound these days. Do you know why? Because we've had such enormous technical successes. We feel like masters of the world. With all this humanism we don't bother much about heaven and eternity.

But we are in a sense like unborn infants. The eye that is being formed in the mother's womb has never seen the light. The ear has never heard the sounds of the world, and the brain has not thought as you're

66

thinking now. The unborn infant has no concept of the world he will soon inhabit.

We are developing, but are we "in the know"? A scientist says that when he's worked for years unlocking one door, six more locked doors appear before him. Or the Bible says: "At present we are men looking at puzzling reflections in a mirror. The time will come when we shall see reality whole and face to face! At present all I know is a little fraction of the truth."[1]

A God who would create persons only to destroy them, would be as monstrous as a man who generates life in order to destroy it before it issues forth from the womb. (I'm not about to discuss abortion with you, but what monster would want to bring in life only to cause an abortion? Besides, why do people feel so very guilty after they have aborted? Isn't that an indication that life and not death is our destiny?)

"But," and you were leaning forward as you talked earnestly trying to get some answers, "most of you Christians do all this for what's in it for you. Don't you work for rewards? You're not worried about the dirty now-and-now. All you look for is the sweet by-and-by. But if you are working for heavenly medals, isn't that an underhanded motive? Is that even the right thing to do?"

Well now, that isn't quite correct about the dirty now-and-now. True enough, some Christians have been otherworldly. But Christianity has never neglected involvement with the world. It just isn't historically accurate. Those who were on their way to heaven left their marks on the earth.

What about hospitals? Humanitarian efforts? The end of slavery and child labor? What of today's concern about war, poverty and racial equality? Isn't it precisely because of Christianity that men have been free to explore, to improve, to discover and to benefit mankind? Are not all our social programs the result of Western civilization, and isn't Western civilization the product of Christianity? Where do you see any of this in the East? Have the religions of the East built hospitals and retirement homes for the elderly?

T.S. Eliot says that we are a Christian culture. He means by this that Western civilization is the product of Christianity. He also warns us that if Christianity should ever go, the whole of our culture will go with it!

Otherworldly? Hardly. I don't think that charge will stick. Many Christians are concerned about this world in our day, and they are often roundly criticized for it.

Now what about this bid for compensation? You are right—Jesus spoke about rewards. He was quite emphatic too. We can't get away from that. So let me face your charge head on.

"Beware of doing your good deeds conspicuously to catch men's eyes or you will miss the reward of your Heavenly Father," said Jesus.[2] So there will be rewards in heaven. Jesus went on to illustrate. One person contributed to charity in order to impress people. People noticed, and he received praise. But when you do a good deed, He said, "don't even let your left hand know what your right hand is doing, so that your giving may be secret. Your Father who sees all secrets will reward you."[3]

A spiritual man arrested people by his prayers. He was recognized also. People considered him a spiritual giant. "But when you pray, go into your own room, shut your door and pray to your Father privately. Your Father who sees all private things will reward you."[4]

Another sacrificed and told everyone about his great sacrifices. He also received recognition. But "when you fast, brush your hair and wash your face so that nobody knows that you are fasting—let it be a secret between

68

you and your Father. And your Father who knows all secrets will reward you."[5]

So, I cannot escape the fact that Jesus spoke about rewards. Now the question is—do we consciously work for recognition? Is this why we are "good" Christians? What if there were no crowns—would we chuck the whole thing?

"That's it. I think many would. They'd drop it, if only they were not afraid to. What if there is nothing to it? No rewards. No heaven. No crowns. No wings. No harps. Nothing at all?"

Oh. Let me return to this question of rewards in just a moment. Let's first talk about wings and crowns and harps.

"Yes, and streets of gold and pearly gates. . . ."

Where do you find all this in the Bible? It's in the book of Revelation, the last book of the Bible. Now that book is full of symbolism, and you must understand it like that. There's a good reason for it.

John wrote it in code for Christians, so that *they* would grasp it, but not the Romans. It was a kind of underground paper. John wrote it to disguise the message for outsiders, since Christians can decipher the code. Unless you see this, you will surely misread the book of Revelation.

For example, Jesus is spoken of as the Lamb. Christians understand Jesus to be the Lamb of God, who takes away the sin of the world.[6] For them John pictures a lamb on the throne of the universe. Not an *actual* lamb, obviously. The point is that Jesus is on the throne, not Caesar! John did not dare to say that out loud. It would have sounded subversive. A Christian found in possession of such a revolutionary paper could lose his head.

Streets of gold? Better even than the Roman roads! Besides, what is more enduring or valuable? Harps?

69

That throws this matter of rewards into a different perspective. "The man who wants to save his life will lose it; but the man who loses his life for my sake will find it," said Jesus.[7] Those who attempt to preserve their own lives (by living for honors) will in the end lose everything. But those who throw away their lives in service of God and man will be saved.

I want to underline those words "for My sake." They make Christian living unique. They do not counsel good for goodness' sake, as the idealist proposes. It's for Jesus' sake. He explains Himself what this means in the parable of the sheep and goats. They are divided on the basis of their works.

But those who fed the hungry, clothed the naked and visited the sick were actually doing more: "I assure you that whatever you did for the humblest of my brothers you did for me."[8] Not for reward. Not for self. But for Him and His creation—man. It was a response, a response of faith to the love of God in Christ.

And when you come right down to it, this parable with its rewards of eternal life, isn't really about pie-in-the-sky-by-and-by. It's all about action in the dirty here and now.

Notes

[1] I Corinthians 13:12
[2] Matthew 6:1
[3] Matthew 6:3,4
[4] Matthew 6:6
[5] Matthew 6:17,18
[6] John 1:29
[7] Matthew 16:25
[8] Matthew 25:40

72

CHAPTER 10

I Don't Know
What You Mean by "Holy Spirit"

Sooner or later in our conversation you are likely to turn to me with a question, which often arises just about the time you've faced some of the main tenets of Christianity. And then you attack from another direction. It goes something like this: "If I'm to believe in God, I could perhaps believe in one God. Like the Jews and others. But why do Christians accept three gods? The Trinity bothers me. God the Father, the Son and the Holy Spirit. That's confusing. I can't understand it. It doesn't make sense to me. Do you actually believe in the Trinity?"

Yes, the Trinity. You aren't the only one who gets hung up on that. And I don't think anyone can fully explain it. I won't drag out those old arguments about the three-in-one, although they help some people. You

73

know, like the formula H_2O. This represents water as liquid or frozen or as steam. But it's still H_2O. Time is made up of the past, present and future. Three-in-one. A cube remains one cube even though it has six sides.

What you have to get straight in spite of all this three-in-one formula, is that Christians believe not in three gods but in one. Only one. Consider that the writers of the New Testament did not find themselves incompatible with the Old Testament. Yet this one God has revealed Himself as Father, Son and Holy Spirit. He is both Creator and Redeemer, both Almighty and Incarnate (which means God in human flesh).

A person can show three or more sides of himself. I am a husband to my wife, a father to my children, a preacher to a congregation, a writer to readers. But I remain one person.

Now that's as far as I'm answering your question. I'm about to bypass this doctrine, to cut you off. Does this surprise you? You know that I'm not in the habit of avoiding issues. Let me explain. I don't think we should argue the doctrine of the Trinity. No one becomes a Christian because of the Trinity. That's the wrong approach. That's why you don't find the early Christians preaching the doctrine of the Trinity.

Actually, in the fourth and fifth centuries Christians spent a great deal of time on this. Gregory of Nazianzus was a writer of creeds which attempted to define the Trinity in words. He was dubbed "the theologian" by his peers, and he confessed: "It is difficult to conceive God but to define Him in words is an impossibility. In my opinion it is impossible to express Him, and yet more impossible to conceive Him."

You see, the Trinity became a *Christian* problem. Christians must wrestle with it, but it's not really your concern. Why not? Because all you have to consider is the Person of Jesus. Who is He? What did He do?

74

What did He say? And what happened to Him? After you come to grips with this issue—who is Jesus?—you are forced to formulate a doctrine of God.

If you accept Jesus as the Son of God, equal with God, God in the world, God become flesh, then you run smack into the problem of the Trinity. For the Father was in heaven, while Jesus (the Son) prayed to Him. So there you are. And that's a Christian problem. All those early creeds are attempts at clarification of the profound truth: "God was in Christ personally reconciling the world to himself."[1] Add to this the Holy Spirit and you are faced with three, one, or three-in-one.

"All right. There's another problem for me. What in the world do you mean by Holy Spirit? I can understand in a way about God and Jesus. But this really gets me. I don't know what you mean by 'Holy Spirit.'"

That question is straight to the point, and I won't cut you off on it. Let's begin this way. Too many Christians have a religion about God and Jesus Christ, and never consider the Spirit at all. Do you know anything about the Pentecostal movement?

"You mean those Christians who shout and clap and whoop it up? The emotional types? The holy rollers and the sawdust trail and all that hallelujah?"

Yes, in a way, but not exactly. I admit some of them carry on at times, but my point is this. Pentecostalism arose because too many of the denominations neglected to emphasize the Holy Spirit. They stress a religion of experience, something that is happening *now*. Jesus is present. He is with us in His Spirit. They're not all that emotional, but they believe in a personal experience of God.

Don't get the idea that this emphasis on the Spirit is confined to the Pentecostals. Far from it. They have

75

brought a corrective that has led many to realize that God is Father and Son *and* Holy Spirit.

You see, you can vaguely believe in Almighty God. He's upstairs looking over the whole business. You can consider Jesus a good man, who lived two thousand years ago and went about doing good. All that's quite comfortable.

It doesn't mean too much. Now that you have that figured out, you can turn back to your television. You've been to church, you've worshiped a faraway God and a nice Jesus. Besides, television is more exciting than religion anyway.

But if you want to find meaning, purpose, experience, a change in your thoughts and actions, then you arrive at the Holy Spirit. That is, God present with us. Not up there in the sky. Not back there in the Bible lands. But right here and right now, capable of revolutionizing your life. That's what we mean by the Holy Spirit.

Boris Pasternak wrote in Dr. Zhivago: "If the beast who sleeps in man could be held down by threats—any kind of threats . . . then the highest emblem of humanity would be the lion tamer in the circus with his whip. . . . But don't you see, this is just the point—what has for centuries raised man above the beast is not the cudgel but an inward music: the irresistible power of unarmed truth." That's a poetic way of speaking of the inner power, God's Spirit in man.

Now let's see how this works out in real life. Remember those disciples of Jesus? After His crucifixion they were discouraged, and even after they saw the risen Christ, they returned into Galilee to the old familiar routines. They actually went back to fishing. They did! Even though they had seen the risen Christ! Nothing wrong with fishing, of course, or earning a living. But think of it: They had just witnessed the greatest event in the history of the world—God in human flesh, dying on a cross, rising from the dead. And then to go back to fishing . . . ?

Incidently, isn't that another note of honesty in the Bible? The apostles recorded their own failures.

Then Jesus appeared to them, encouraged them, and promised them power. They certainly needed something. Had they stayed at their fishing business, we would never have heard of Christianity! But somehow or other, they left their nets again and went to Jerusalem. There they met together for ten days and waited for this promise of power.

And then it happened: "When the actual day of Pentecost came they were all assembled together. Suddenly there was a sound from heaven like the rushing of a violent wind, and it filled the whole house where they were seated. Before their eyes appeared tongues like flames, which separated off and settled above the head of each one of them. They were all filled with the Holy Spirit and began to speak in different languages as the Spirit gave them power to proclaim his Message."[2]

These same cowardly disciples now stand up and proclaim Jesus to the Jews, who have gathered for this feast of Pentecost. Their boldness brings three thousand Jews into Christianity in one day. Think about that! No one sermon has that much persuasive power— not among the Jews anyway. This is the work of the Holy Spirit. Religion has become real. It is no longer theory but experience. It changes cowards into men of courage, fishermen into men who fish for God's sake.

That's the question you have to face. What in the world changed those men? Something did. What? The New Testament speaks basically of two miracles: the resurrection of Jesus and the transformation of human nature by the Spirit of God.

Does this help you to see how the Holy Spirit works? To realize why we confess that the one and only God has revealed Himself as Father, Son and Holy Spirit?

"But if that's true," you say, "then Christians should be far better than other people. If they have the Spirit of God, that is. And that I don't see at all. Christians aren't that good. And what about all the bloodshed in history by the church, the Crusades, the Inquisition and the awful things done in the name of Christ? What about all the race prejudice of modern times? How can you even speak of a Holy Spirit when you look at Christendom?"

This entire question about the church, the Crusades, the Inquisition and race hatred we will tackle next time for sure. It's a big question. But you ask why Christians aren't much better than other people.

Obviously Christians should be better, if they have received the Spirit of God. But perhaps they didn't have as much to begin with. (We do not all have the same IQ either.) It's easy enough to make generalizations. Suppose you pick two individuals and compare them. But hold on. Are you sufficiently informed about them to make such a comparison? What do you actually know of their inner struggles and battles?

Of course if anyone is looking for an argument against Christianity, he can very easily latch onto this one. It may be that you're searching for arguments, when you are beginning to fear that Christianity may be true after all.

No, Christians don't become perfect automatically because they have received the Spirit. But how else could they begin to live as Christians? Suppose I had to write Shakespearean drama. How could I do this, unless in some way the genius of Shakespeare were given to me? So, there are gifts of the Spirit. "The Spirit . . . produces in human life fruits such as these: love, joy,

78

peace, patience, kindness, generosity, fidelity, tolerance and self-control."[3]

A Christian is open to God's Spirit. He knows he cannot produce this new life by himself; he allows God to produce it in him. It's a daily affair. It has to be worked out every day anew.

But there's something else to be said. Have you become aware of what people around you are saying? They say: "The world needs a new spirit." As if there is a choice, an assortment of spirits to choose from. But it is a *spirit* that is to bring the change.

Now the fundamental change through the Holy Spirit comes in the *direction* of our lives. You are looking for a change in our *speed*. You want us to go faster, to have more power. But what if we were like an old clunker which couldn't make it up to sixty-five. At least we're now headed down the right road! Christians cannot live for themselves any longer, for materialistic goals and mere pleasure. There are new goals, God-given goals, goals that move us toward God and man.

Of course we keep on making mistakes. Even the best of us. Not just little mistakes either. Big ones. We may, in fact, be blind to our own mistakes, but there will be times when we are caught up short. Just as when a police car pulls you over to the side of the road, and he points out an infraction of the law which you know you've been guilty of time and again.

We wish it didn't have to be like that, that we could just have perfection poured into us. Instant perfection, like instant coffee.

I'm not about to minimize these mistakes. Far from it. We are constantly told in the New Testament to live in the Spirit, to walk in the Spirit, to be filled with the Spirit. It's a lifelong process, and you can see why it's necessary.

Perhaps this will become clearer to you when I tell

you that you're being drawn toward Christ by this same Spirit. I know what that sounds like to you. Before I became a Christian, they said it to me. I raised my eyebrows and thought they were a bit cracked in the head. Now I know that Jesus had this to say: (He was speaking of the Spirit) "When he comes, he will convince the world of the meaning of sin, of true goodness and of judgment. He will expose their sin because they do not believe in me; he will reveal true goodness . . . and he will show them the meaning of judgment."[4]

This means you are being courted, enlightened and convicted by the Spirit of God. You are not aware of this, but are you perhaps aware of some inner frustration, a loss of meaning, a sense of boredom or loneliness? This is how the Holy Spirit convinces you of the emptiness of life apart from God. His whole purpose is to "guide you into everything that is true."[5]

But in the last analysis you're not supposed to look at a Spirit. You're supposed to let Him live in and through you. Look at Jesus. Then His Spirit will truly arise within you. What else do you think Jesus implied when He said at the very last, "Remember, I am with you always, to the end of the world."[6]

Notes

[1]II Corinthians 5:19
[2]Acts 2:1–4
[3]Galatians 5:22,23
[4]John 16:8–11
[5]John 16:13
[6]Matthew 28:20

CHAPTER 11

Why Bother with the Church?

Well, we finally have to face it. This is the question you've been asking from the beginning. Why the church? Why bother with the church? Why can't you just believe in God, live a good life and forget about church?

I must warn you right now that I may not be able to muster persuasive replies to answer you, or to white-wash both our long history of failure and sin and the enigma we see in today's institution. So, tell me your question again.

"For one thing I can't reconcile the bloody wars fought by the church. How can the church make war when Christ teaches peace and turning the other cheek? On that basis how do you explain the Crusades, the Inquisition, the gas chambers in Germany and race

81

prejudice in the United States? Is this Christianity? Is this love? Is this following the teaching of Jesus?"

All right. You do realize, don't you, that your question is based on this premise: you presume that the teaching of Jesus should make a difference, and that Christians ought to live differently. Wasn't it the philosopher Nietzsche who said that if Christians would look (and behave) more redeemed, he could believe in their Redeemer? Gandhi also complained about Christians. They stood between him and faith in Christ. He believed in the teachings of Jesus *in spite of* Christians. He said that the first thing we ought to do is live more like Jesus.

"What about the Crusades?"

The church is hardly in a position to defend the Crusades today. Perhaps the only question we could raise is, What motivated them? Why did the Crusaders travel to the land of Israel (or, as it was then called, Palestine)? They went in quest of holy things. They went in hope of recapturing those places where Jesus walked, to rescue them from "the heathen." The vision of Jerusalem drove them on.

Their main purpose was not to kill, but to rescue and recapture. It didn't turn out that way, of course. There can be no defense for the vicious battles and bloodshed which ensued. There surely could have been another way.

I know that isn't very satisfactory. There is no real answer. I can't defend the Crusades any more than I could represent a guilty criminal in court.

"Can you explain the Inquisition any better?"

Now that took place after the Reformation. There is some confusion about the Inquisition, since it was largely a persecution executed by one branch of the Christian church—the Roman Catholic Church. They persecuted the Jews, for which they found political, social and economic reasons, but we could hardly call them Christian reasons. But I must add hastily that many conscientious Catholics deeply regret this action of their church.

Nor can I whitewash all Protestants. I won't attempt it, because then you'll throw the witch trials at me. And that happened in so-called Christian America.

"Since you brought that up, what about the Protestants?" (You're eager to jump right into that issue.) "Why the Salem trials and burning of witches? What kind of inhumanity was that?"

I told you that I can't excuse it. The only point I can raise is one of interpretation. These people, with a different approach, misrepresented Scripture. Isn't it possible that they misinterpreted God's will in this? "Misinterpreted" is too mild a word for it, I agree. But they received their guidance from the Old Testament, not from the words of Jesus.

Still, are we so much better than they? The only reason we don't hunt witches today is that we don't believe in them. We do hunt spies and traitors. Besides, we sacrifice young men in often meaningless wars. Is there any defense for that?

You know, all of these questions deal with the past. What about the present?

"OK. Let's come to the present. Then you face the greatest horror of all—the murder of six million Jews in the gas chambers of a supposedly Christian Germany."

Yes. What happened under Hitler in the gas chambers can't actually be charged to the Christian church. It was the work of a fanatical maniac, who was far from being a Christian.

"But the church allowed it. People simply turned their backs. They pretended not to notice anything."

You have a point there. It all happened in an enlightened, so-called Christian nation. Some must have turned their heads. Others, I'm sure, never knew what was happening. Like the vast majority they didn't care to know. But there were Christians who rebelled. Men like Martin Niemoller and Dietrich Bonhoeffer were thrown into prison. They stood up against this inhumanity. Those who knew what was taking place suffered severely.

"But all that didn't stop the slaughter. And now we have race riots in the U.S.A because of all our prejudice, bigotry and second-class citizenship. How can the church call itself Christian when it has produced a Ku Klux Klan? What of those who preach the superiority of white American Protestants? And you ask me to become a Christian?"

What you have reference to is far from "Christian." Such preachers of white superiority do more harm than good. There's no excuse for the K.K.K. I don't see how you can associate this with Christianity any more than you can associate blatant pornography with legitimate literature. All you say is true—about the Crusades, the Inquisition, the witch trials and race prejudice. One thing for sure, none of it can be identified with Jesus of Nazareth.

Of course it makes you wonder how anyone like that can associate himself with Jesus. But, then, Jesus Himself warned us about such people: "It is not everyone who keeps saying to me 'Lord, Lord' who will enter the Kingdom of Heaven. . . . In 'that day' many will say to me, 'Lord, Lord, didn't we preach in your name, didn't we cast out devils in your name, and do many great things in your name?' Then I shall tell them plainly: 'I have never known you. Go away from me; you have worked on the side of evil!' "[1]

The point I'm making is that this is entirely possible. Perhaps it even sheds light on some of the questions you've raised.

84

But to return. Let me admit it. There are those who call themselves Christians who still retain race prejudice. They shouldn't, but they do. Others may hold resentments. Still others are gossipy. And there are those with unforgiving tempers. Should I mention pride, even spiritual pride? I could go on. We can't sanction any of this. But who is perfect? Who of us can judge another? Is there anyone on the face of the earth who has this right, who has risen above every form of evil?

"No, that's true. Still it bothers me that there are many people who are not Christians, and who are not prejudiced. They live better. They are more human. They put Christians to shame by their lives and attitudes. What do you have to say about that?"

I can only say that it probably bothers me as much (if not more) than it bothers you. It bothers me very much that there are Christians who have race prejudice. But it also bothers me that there are proud Christians, self-centered Christians, loveless Christians, critical Christians, lustful Christians and temperamental Christians. Only I have to remember (as I said a moment ago) that I'm not so great that I can judge them. I've got myself on my hands—and that's enough!

Let me tell you about a great Christian of our time. He is a German with a conscience, a preacher who reaches a congregation of over four thousand regularly. Helmut Thielicke has in one of his books admitted from the inside all that you see amiss from the outside.

"If I were not convinced that Christ is risen and that he lives . . . I probably could not have drawn any other conclusion except that of leaving the church," he says. Now, mind you, that's a devout and honest theologian talking. He suffers *for* the church, but he suffers *in* the church.

"Would not then the one legitimate form in which one may preach and missionize today be to speak in this way of suffering because of the church? Is it not possible that this kind of honest proclamation would make people stop and listen? . . . Could not such a confession prompt people to ask *what* it is that is still worth loving in it and that more than outweighs our suffering and trouble with it?"[2]

I'm aware that this is not an answer either. But it does put you on a different plane from which to view the problem. Isn't it clear that many of us inside the church are equally pained with our hypocrisies and mistakes? We wish we could present a spotless record, but we can't. And we can't wipe the record clean either. Perhaps that's the trouble with the church. It's a human institution. It's made up of men—sinful, proud and earthy men who nevertheless profess to believe in Jesus Christ.

"It isn't good enough for me," you say. "These are not answers. Nor are they good reasons for me to become a Christian. You'll have to do better than that. I feel like the man who said he believed in God but not in His ground crew."

All right. But before I change my tune, consider this. Doesn't it mean anything to you that there are those within the church who are deeply affected by our failures? Haven't you observed some very good attempts by Christians to counteract our errors? Are you not aware that many church leaders have bemoaned the prejudices of the church? Haven't you read the stories of ministers who've spoken out and been relieved of their pulpits?

So, why not look at the positive side of Christianity? You surely know some people yourself who are devout, who live the life, who are examples of compassion and concern. Don't you know anyone who admits to the scandal of the church?

And yet you do not judge music by its latest expression. You remember that there are symphonies by Beethoven and sonatas by Mozart. You do not evaluate architecture by the hot dog stand on the corner. You know there are cathedrals. Nor do you criticize bankers because some have embezzled funds. You still put your money in the bank. The same goes for the medical profession, in spite of some charlatans.

Why then judge the Christian church by those poor examples? Why not take some good examples, like the good Samaritan instead of all the bad Samaritans you focus on? Besides, you know there was a Jesus. And I keep on saying to you, consider Him.

"But even going to church bothers me. I look at those people; they don't look like Christians."

What are Christians supposed to look like?

"I mean they're cliquish or they talk a lot before the service begins or they do funny things. And then I don't get much out of the service. So I don't go anymore. I just can't see why the church is necessary."

The services don't mean much to you. I can understand that. Sometimes that's *your* fault, but sometimes it's the fault of the preacher. Some of them can be incredibly dull. I don't know why. They've got the biggest piece of news in the whole world, but they can't seem to get more excited about it than if they were reading the phone book. I don't think they realize they're talking to people who want to be helped, who are eager to know the good news, and who want to find God. (Of course sometimes there are other reasons why people are in church, too.)

Suppose you were on a trip in Europe and while in Paris took the elevator up the Eiffel Tower. There's quite a view from the top. But on this day when you get up there, the fog is as thick as pea soup. You can't see your hand in front of your nose. Does that mean

87

there's no view? Not at all. The view is there all the same and it's magnificent.

That's how it may seem to you when you enter a church. You could get an impressive view like the prophet Isaiah. One day in the Temple he had a vision of God. It changed his life. John Wesley was transformed because of a worship experience in a little Moravian church.

Just because you can't see anything on a foggy day doesn't mean there's nothing to see. Maybe the fog has to lift and then you will see the value and beauty of worship. "Open thou mine eyes, that I may behold wondrous things out of thy law,"[3] prayed the psalmist and then added the assurance: "The LORD is nigh unto all them that call upon him, to all that call upon him in truth."[4]

Worship is more than one of the recent dolls which have been made available for children, a doll that acquires a tan in the sun and loses it again after some hours indoors. Worship is not momentary, an outward glow. It is something inward and deep.

Let's sum it up. What we've really been saying is that Christians aren't perfect. They are in a battle. They experience continual struggle. "The whole energy of the lower nature is set against the Spirit, while the whole power of the Spirit is contrary to the lower nature. Here is the conflict, and that is why you are not free to do what you want to do. The activities of the lower nature are obvious. . . . (But) those who belong to Christ Jesus have crucified their old nature with all that it loved and lusted for."[5]

We are human. And we remain human. God's Spirit is within us. We are to walk and live in that Spirit daily. There is no perfect church, but you will discover those who, in spite of their painful weaknesses, desire to walk with Jesus.

Only a man who hasn't learned how to count is free from math problems. Only a man who is asleep is free from life's struggles. Those who are awake find conflict —and reality.

Look at Jesus. Ask yourself what He wants of you. That's a much better road to take. Do you suppose *He* wants you to become a Christian?

Notes

[1]Matthew 7:21–23
[2]Helmut Thielicke, *The Trouble with the Church* (New York: Harper & Row, 1965). Used by permission.
[3]Psalm 119:18
[4]Psalm 145:18
[5]Galatians 5:17,19,24

CHAPTER 12

Man Isn't Really So Bad!

"You Christians are always talking about man as a sinner. He's bad, you say. He's no good. I can't buy that. I don't think people are so terrible. I have a better outlook on humanity. There's a lot of good in people. Besides, if you go around telling people they're sinners, they'll act like sinners. If you tell them they're good, they'll be good. You've got it all mixed up. And you give people the idea that God is against all fun."

You know, I used to think much like you. I never heard the word *sin* until Christians started using it on me. Then I conjured up visions of what went on downtown in burlesque houses, strip joints, grimy bars and "those kinds of places." That was sin, but, of course, that didn't touch me. I wasn't a sinner like that, and I tried to be good. I had myself firmly convinced on that score.

But in a way you're wrong to assume that if you tell people they're sinners they'll act like sinners, and if you tell them they're good they'll be good. We are what we are. Some Christians who continually convince themselves about sin, don't think *they* are so bad anyway. All the others are. They're not, even though they use the word *sin* more than anyone else.

Let's get to your real question. What is man—good or bad? Now does it have to be one or the other? Does it have to be black or white? It's not as clear-cut as all that. Man is a mixture, a mixture of good and evil.

If you believe that man is inherently good, it becomes so easy to point out all the evil he has created. Just look at the world. It's hardly a paradise. You don't have to point to crime syndicates, juvenile delinquency, unhappy homes, gambling, alcoholism, drug addiction, mental illness or the wars men cannot seem to stop fighting. Misery is everywhere.

Man is good? The record refutes it. "Man was made a little lower than the angels," commented Mark Twain on Psalm 8, "and he's sinking lower all the time."

If, on the other hand, you attempt to paint the portrait of man as totally depraved, you easily discover points on the credit side. You can always refer to a good deed performed by some good Samaritan. You can consider the crime fighters, social workers, patient teachers and all the countless "little" people who silently help and heal. Perhaps you will be able to point to someone in your own circle, who's been good to you and gone out of the way for you.

I should clear up one point in Christian theology. By total depravity we do not imply that man is totally evil,

91

but that the total man is evil. His will, emotions, body, mind, motivations, imagination—*everything* has been touched by evil. Every part has been affected.

Man is not black or white. He's a mixture. He is as far from perfection on the one end, as he is from complete corruption on the other. But, of course, some are nearer the one extreme than the other. Now how can this be so?

The biblical account of creation gives an obvious answer. If you accept the fact that God created man, then you know that we were made in the image of God. But something happened. Man rebelled against his Creator. He determined to be his own boss, to call his own shots, to take matters into his own hands. That's how he disobeyed, and he fell from his good beginning.

"I can't accept that story of Adam and Eve."

Fair enough. Can you accept these words of Robert Louis Stevenson: "To touch the heart of the mystery, we find in him (man) one thought, strange to the point of lunacy, the thought of duty, the thought of something owing to himself, to his neighbor, to his God. An ideal of decency to which he would rise if it were possible. A limit of shame below which, if it were possible, he will not stoop."

The question is, from where did man get this ideal? And, where did he get this limit of shame? Christians say that because *God* created man, this is where it came from. Whether you accept the story of Adam and Eve or not, it's plain to see that man retains within himself some traces of the good. Yet he is bent toward evil . . . !

While rebelling against this Christian idea, one girl said: "I like my friends, but I hate mankind." Why? You see? That's the confusion. Man is like this, and it won't do to argue with the French existentialist Albert

Camus that man is out of joint because the world is out of joint. Camus never faces the obvious question: *Why is the world out of joint?* What happened? What makes the world so inhuman?

When a mirror crashes, it breaks into a thousand pieces. The mirror is still represented by all these pieces, but it's not usable anymore. So the image of God has been broken in man. The pieces remain, hence our ability toward goodness. But something else has happened too. And we can't ignore it, just as we can't ignore a strange growth in our body.

Have you ever asked yourself why it is, when a person runs with the wrong crowd, it's suddenly so much easier to do something wrong? Why is it when he gets close enough to some temptation that it doesn't seem so bad, while when he was looking at it from a distance, he wouldn't touch it? Why is it when the price is right, we can be bought? I don't know what your moral problems are, but I'm sure you have them. Like the rest of us.

Now, what really counts in life is the comeback. Every one of us has to make a comeback. So you've fumbled. Can you recover your fumble? Can you pick up the ball and start running again? And this recovery is about as tough as life becomes. It means confession, restitution, forgiveness, reconciliation.

"I still don't see what good it does for the church to call people sinners. Why don't you just preach the good news? Why tell people they're bad?"

That isn't the only thing we say about man. But consider your alternative. What does it leave you? On the one hand you say that evil doesn't count. Man isn't to blame. He's not responsible. He won't have to pay for it. There'll be no judgment. On the other hand you have to believe man can save himself. He's good enough. He'll make it without anyone's help.

"Look," said a young fellow to me, "I'll simply say to God that I've done my best. That's all He can expect. Sure I'm not perfect. But I've tried. And I'm as good as anyone else. I don't think," he concluded wistfully, "that God will turn me down." Which means, you see, that our faults don't matter too much, and we're good enough to make it to heaven on our own.

"But what about Jesus? He didn't go around calling everybody sinners, did He?"

That's true. Not everybody. He never called attention to it, except as far as religious people were concerned. When a woman had been taken in adultery, others said she was a sinner, but He didn't. She knew that already. She did not consider herself worthy. He did not condone her sin, but He accepted her and told her to go and sin no more.

When it came to those good, religious people, Jesus called them hypocrites, whited sepulchres, snakes, and even the children of the devil. They were very self-righteous, and they needed to see themselves as they actually were in the sight of God.

Those who know they are sinners need only to hear the good news of forgiveness. Those who pretend they are not—even though they may talk about sin all the time—need to be brought up short. Christianity has nothing much to say to people who think they're very good. It only begins to talk to those who admit there's something wrong.

A Christian physician points out in comparing men and women, that men especially are conscious of their sins—sexual lust, cheating in business, excessive pride in their work, and so on. Because of this, says Dr. Paul Tournier, a man hesitates about going to church and parading his piety. He feels he can't set it right like that, and he doesn't want to be a hypocrite. Is this the reason why you hesitate to be seen in church?

"I've never really thought about it that way. I'll have to think about it," you say with that characteristic honesty of yours. "But is that all you can tell me? Man is a mixture? Christian people too, I presume. At least they're no different from other people. They have good and bad qualities too."

Exactly. Christianity is just one beggar telling another beggar where the bread is to be found (Daniel T. Niles). We are all beggars. We're on the same footing. Not, "I know the answers and you don't." Not, "I'm a good Christian and you're a bad sinner." Not, "I'm going to tell you what you must do to become like me." No, not that.

One beggar tells another. We're all in the same boat. I've got my hands open too, like any beggar. My hands are open to God, in order that I may receive His mercy and grace. If I kept a closed fist, I wouldn't receive anything. God's not able to put anything into a clenched fist. If I held my hand behind my back with something in it, that would be useless too.

But since I'm a beggar with you, I can tell you I've been given—bread. The Bread of Life. Nourishing. Sustaining. And you can taste it too. All it takes is a willingness to hold your hand out. . . .

So, man is not merely good or bad. He is redeemable. He has the potential of salvation. He can find life through Christ.

Probably the most famous story Jesus ever told was about a boy who asked his father for his inheritance. He went to a distant country and lived it up. He wanted his freedom, and he got it.

There in that country, far away from his father's house, life went along well. But soon his funds ran out and when that happened his friends dropped him like a hot potato. He found himself alone in the world, and without any job. He finally sank so low that he was eating food generally thrown to pigs.

You catch on now? Of course. You recognize the story as the parable of the prodigal son.[1]

Then something happened to him. He came to his senses. He began to think. His freedom wasn't all it was cracked up to be. And he found himself remembering his father and home.

Jean-Paul Sartre once said: "I find that I am alive and it sickens me." Perhaps the prodigal felt that way too. But he added something else: "I will arise and go to my father. Things are better at home." And his memory of home became so strong that he picked himself up and went back.

That meant he was redeemable. He could go home! And what a surprise awaited him there. His father had been looking for him. His father came running toward him, hugged him, kissed him and welcomed him. The son went into his prepared speech.

"Father, I have done wrong in the sight of Heaven and in your eyes. I don't deserve to be called your son anymore. . . ." But his father cut him short. He wasn't interested in it. His son had come back. That was all that mattered. He received him joyfully and showered him with gifts. He threw a big feast. He killed the fatted calf and placed his son at his right hand at dinner.

Not only is this the story of the prodigal son and his redeemability, it convincingly demonstrates the love of God. That father represents God, the compassion and concern of God. Our Father eagerly welcomes us home.

This is the story of man, you know. Created by God, nourished in the father's house, and then rebelliously running away into a far country. Living it up for self and personal advantage, and learning that it doesn't pay. It isn't freedom after all, but slavery to (may I use the word now?) sin. And then, repenting, hopefully picking up the pieces and coming back to the Father.

"But what if I believed this once? What if years ago I accepted it and turned to God? What if I've gone back again into the far country? What hope is there for me now?"

There was a cartoon in the *New Yorker* magazine picturing a banquet full of guests and servants. The table was loaded with a roast and good food. The host stood up to carve. He turned to his right where his son sat in the place of honor and said: "After all, son, this is the *fourth* fatted calf!"

This is the story of man. Man, who always longs for that far-off country; man, who always rebels against God. Why? Because by nature this is what he is. He is always returning too, and then he is received by his compassionate Father. Of course that's the way it is, both painful and joyous. But with all that, this mixture of good and evil can be redeemed. And that's the good news Jesus brings.

So I ask you, are you willing to say: "I will arise and go to my Father"? Why not? What other alternative do you really have?

Notes

1Luke 15:11-24

97

CHAPTER 13

What Do You See in the Cross?

If we were to omit the crucifixion of Jesus from our conversation, we would be politely bypassing the central issue of the Christian faith. The cross has already come up in our talks, and you know that Christians have always placed great emphasis on the death of Jesus. The cross is the symbol of Christianity.

"I know that's true," you say, "but I can't understand it really. Why all this preoccupation with the death of Jesus? Why don't you talk more about His life? Isn't it important what Jesus taught, what He did and how He lived? Why center everything in that cross?"

It's true, isn't it, that when we remember the great men of history that we praise their lives and accomplishments. The founders of all other religions are re-

98

membered for their teachings, not their deaths. Only Christianity points to a symbol of death.

And it's *not* because Jesus was the only one to die in the prime of life. Moses died at a ripe, old age. Buddha died when past eighty, surrounded by his favorite disciples. Confucius was over seventy when he passed away in peace. Mohammed, over sixty, reclining on the breast of his wife, died revered and respected. Only Jesus, after a short ministry in the full strength of His manhood, was betrayed, deserted, condemned and crucified. He died as a criminal between two thieves.

Now, why this concern about His death? It's certainly not because His life was uneventful or His teaching unimportant. To the contrary. Everything He said and did is of utmost significance, and the church has been at fault when they've tended to overlook His life and teaching.

But even when you consider what Jesus taught, you are faced with the cross. He warned His disciples that He would be crucified, and that if they wanted to come after Him, they'd have to take up their cross too.

"But many men have died. Some have suffered a far worse death than crucifixion. Why make the crucifixion of Jesus so special?"

Perhaps there's a clue in these words of Jesus: "I lay down my life. . . . No one is taking it from me, but I lay it down of my own free will. I have the power to lay it down and I have the power to take it up again."[1] He voluntarily laid down His life. He did it willingly. He was not being forced.

It is easier to suffer because of an order than to suffer voluntarily. It is also easier to suffer with others than to suffer alone. And it is easier to suffer physically than spiritually. Yet Jesus suffered freely; He suffered alone, forsaken by His friends; He endured spiritual (as well as physical) agony.

99

You say that others have died on crosses. But *who* dies on this cross? That's the question. Christians affirm that Jesus is not only a man. He is the Eternal in time, God in human flesh. For *Him to die* willingly and voluntarily is—to say the least—shocking! It's actually incomprehensible. It's too much for anyone to grasp. This is not only a man being nailed to the wood. This, then, is God—in the person of His Son—on the cross.

"I see what you're saying, but I don't understand the reason for it. Why did Jesus endure all this, particularly if He knew what was going to happen to Him? Why is all this suffering necessary?"

That's a very important question. Most Christians can only mumble the answer that He died for our sins. But let's see what the cross really means.

Since God has entered this human stream, dying on a cross means that He is going all the way. He who was baptized to identify with us, who lived in poverty and needed to further identify with us, now joins us even at the point of death. How much further could God go?

But let's move beyond that point. Consider what Jesus Himself said about His death: "He began to teach them that it was inevitable that the Son of Man should go through much suffering and be completely repudiated by the elders. . . . The Son of Man must be lifted above the heads of men—as Moses lifted up that serpent in the desert."[2]

Why this inevitability? Why this "must"? What was this great need? Why this divine insistence? If we pursue that question we will get to the meaning of the cross.

"If I understand you now, you're saying that it had to be. Does this imply it was God's demand? Did God insist on the death of Jesus? If you say yes to that, how can I believe in a God of love? I can't understand how a loving God will allow His Son to be put to death!"

There have been Christians who explain the cross as punishment. They believe that God did demand the death of Jesus. I don't like that wording. It does not do justice to God. And it certainly makes it difficult, if not impossible, to believe that love and love alone was behind that sacrifice of the cross.

It was, in fact, redeeming love. Love that takes the punishment itself, love that sacrifices itself. Do you understand this about love? Love is not a safe investment. Love does not guarantee good returns. Love is a risk, it's vulnerable, it can lead to rejection. Your heart may be broken. God's heart was. But that is the risk redeeming love takes.

As to theories about the death of Jesus, they're not important, really. They're explanations. What actually happened is far more important than any theory as to why it happened, or how, or for what reason. And the best way to understand that is to stop analyzing and simply start looking. Meditate on the cross. Let it get under your skin. When you consider *who* suffered there you won't demand any theories, just as you don't ask for explanations in the presence of love.

You see, man has rebelled. He has turned away from God. He's defected. He's turned toward evil and rejected God's will. Or, to put it simply, in spite of some good points, man is a sinner. His whole total self, his body, his mind, his will, his emotions, his motives—*all* have been touched by evil.

"This is a lousy, stinking world," commented a former convict. "I've said this all my life. It's a rough world. That's why I did what I did. I wanted to forget it all. Everybody's out to get you. So I get you before you get me. You gotta take care of yourself."

You understand what he was saying, don't you? Ex-

offers us pardon. He does for man what man cannot do for himself: "God was in Christ personally reconciling the world to himself—not counting their sins against them"![5]

"But I don't want anyone suffering for my sins. I don't want anyone bearing my sins."

"You don't? Are you a parent? Have you ever suffered for your son, ever suffered through all those growing-up pains, suffered because of his inexperience, his stubbornness, his rebellion? What if he didn't want you to suffer because of him?

When my son was quite small, I tried to tell him that I suffered more than he during the times of discipline, but he didn't believe me. One time I struck myself with a stick, to punish myself because of his misbehavior. He broke out in tears. "Don't, Daddy," he cried. "Hit me, but don't hit yourself."

What if God, willing to demonstrate His love for us, did it *this* way? He had attempted other means earlier. He gave the law. He performed miracles. He spoke through prophets. But mankind didn't pay attention. Therefore, the cross. You can't object that He shouldn't have done it. After all, that's *His* decision to make!

So the cross says to us that God's heart was broken, that He cared, that He accepted the responsibility on our behalf. The God of the universe was trampled on! That's the meaning of the cross.

And now you ask me: "Is this all I have to do to become a Christian? Believe this? Don't I have to work away my own sins? Don't I have to do anything else? If that's all there is to it, I must say it sounds too good to be true."

If you want to work for your salvation, how much do you have to do? What production quota will you have to meet? Who establishes the quota? How do you know when it is enough? Is there ever any hope of reaching an end? How can you be sure?

Suppose, on the other hand, Jesus did it all. If that is true, what can there be left to do? If He has done it, there is no need to do anything more. It sounds too good to be true? Of course. But that isn't the whole story.

Look at it like this. I'm drowning and someone offers to help. "No, it's not fair," I cry out. "Don't jump in. Don't risk your life. I'll make it. I don't want your help." But what if I can't possibly make it—what then? Should I keep on refusing help?

That's too simple? But isn't that the meaning of salvation? And we say that Jesus is the *Saviour* of the world.

"What do you have to do?" you ask. Salvation is a gift. You can only receive a gift. You don't work for a gift. But if you accept the gift, aren't you grateful? And doesn't such salvation put you in debt, so to speak, toward the giver? (Not that the giver gives it for that reason. A calculated gift is no gift at all.) But this is true—the greater and more loving the gift, the greater your response and love.

If you have been saved, that will make a profound change in your life. You owe your life to your Saviour.

Well, there's your answer. There's no need to spell it out further. The cross of Jesus, when you are grasped by its wisdom, power and love, becomes the true motivating force for Christian living.

Notes

[1]John 10:17,18
[2]Mark 8:31; John 3:14
[3]Mark 10:45
[4]Isaiah 59:2
[5]II Corinthians 5:19

105

CHAPTER 14

But . . . Resurrection?

If you want to get the full picture, it is inevitable that we bring into focus the one essential and unique proclamation of Christianity, the resurrection of Jesus. Had Jesus merely died, we would probably not have heard of Him. Christianity would have died with Him as simply another sect of Judaism.

Neither would we have dared to speak of Jesus as the Son of God, or greater than other prophets. How could we be sure of His divinity? Then He would remain a good man, an inspiring teacher and a prophet who was unjustly put to death. A terrible death, to be sure. In the prime of life. A great shame.

If this is all there is to Christianity—the life, teaching and untimely death of Jesus, important as these may be—it is still insufficient. I'll even go beyond that and say Christianity is then not demanding of our investigation, nor worthy of our commitment. For even though we affirm that God dwelt among us in human flesh and was crucified, it all ends there in pathetic and despairing defeat.

106

Death vanquishes God. Death is victorious after all. O death, *there* is your sting. O grave, *there* is your victory! God is dead. And, how can a dead God move men to life? Only a living God can command our devotion. The resurrection of Jesus makes the Christian faith unique among all the world's religions. We are not perpetuating a pointless funeral.

"But," you say, "many people have believed in life after death. Consider the Egyptians. They believed in immortality years before Jesus. The Indians looked forward to that happy hunting ground. What's so unique about Christianity's doctrine of heaven?"

I agree. When you put it like that, there's nothing unique about it. Many cultures have believed in life after death. But Christianity sets forth far more. It proclaims a resurrection. And that's as different from immortality as a butterfly is from a cocoon. Resurrection is personal life in a new dimension. Resurrection means that a man came back from the dead. And that never happened in history either before Jesus or since.

That's the great issue. Not merely a hopeful projection of life beyond the grave, but one man breaking through the thick wall of death—bursting through—coming alive with this promise: "Because I am really alive you will be alive. . . . I am coming again to welcome you into my own home, so that you may be where I am."[1]

"But wait a minute," you say. "The New Testament tells stories about Jesus bringing other people back to life. They were supposedly dead. So, how can Jesus be the only one?"

True. We have three such stories in the New Testament. But what happened to these people? As far as we know, they died again. Their being raised must have been a temporary return to this existence. But you probably find these stories difficult to believe (even

107

though they are part of the Gospels), so let's return to the issue.

Jesus' resurrection was not temporary. He did not die again. He rose to live forevermore. The Bible states it this way: "God would not allow the bitter pains of death to touch him. He raised him to life again—and indeed there was nothing by which death could hold such a man."[2]

"How can this be? It sounds fantastic. There isn't any proof of it. Do you want me to believe that a dead man was walking around in Jerusalem? People don't come back from the dead. It isn't logical. It doesn't make sense. If there were a precedent for it, if the great leaders of world religions like Buddha, Moses and Mohammed had risen from the dead, I might consider it. But why only Jesus? Why no one else? This doesn't figure."

Do you realize that you've almost answered your own question? "Why only Jesus?" you ask. Christianity affirms that Jesus is the only begotten Son of God, God present in humanity. This coming of the Saviour, predicted through the Old Testament as the great event of deliverance, only occurred once in the history of the world. Why, then, should any others, even though they were great men, rise from the dead? They were not God. They were prophets and teachers. They did not even hint at being anything more than men. If, however, Jesus is the Son of God, how could death possibly defeat Him?

There's another point in your question. You say it isn't logical, reasonable, scientific. It can't be proved. Did I say it was in that realm? Haven't we again fallen into the trap of *this* world's way of thinking? We want logic, proof. We aren't operating in the realm of logic. Resurrection belongs to another dimension, and you cannot bring scientific measurements to it, anymore

108

than you can measure the density of air with a yard-stick.

Now this doesn't mean that you should park your reason outside and come into our house blindfolded, believing everything. Not at all. There are facts to reckon with, and since we have been taught to live with facts—nothing but facts—let's face a few.

These apostles tell us that they have been with One who rose from the dead. That's a fact, which for them became an experience. Just as there are in life areas which cannot be explained or reasoned out—such as art, beauty, the experience of nature, trusting another person, love—so resurrection is in the realm of experience. And if you'd try to reason it all out, you'd flunk miserably in *life*. Just as you'd flunk out if you attempted to analyze romantic love in courtship by putting it in an IBM machine.

Well, something like this happened to the disciples. They saw a risen Jesus. He who had been with them in life and taken from them in death, was now miraculously alive again—alive forevermore.

They never dreamed that they would have to build a case. That's why they made no attempt to prove it. They simply proceeded to tell their story, the story of what had actually taken place. It sounded incredible, but that was their evidence. Evidence which you can either accept or dismiss.

"But what if it didn't happen? What if they only wished Jesus to be alive again? What if they made themselves believe it? Perhaps it was all a dream. . . ."

Whoever dreamed a dream like that? Do you discover any parallels in other religions or philosophies? Doesn't the very uniqueness in Christianity make it stand out like a sore thumb?

And if they were deceived . . . ? Maybe you can deceive yourself for a while, but would you be willing to

109

put it on the line when it came to imprisonment, torture or death? Some people have, I suppose, died for a delusion. But I cannot imagine this of *all* the disciples. They were not gullible.

Here's another fact. There were more than twelve (eleven if you rule out Judas). One hundred and twenty Christians joined the apostles in a post-resurrection meeting. They waited together for the power Jesus had promised them, the power of His Spirit. Is it conceivable that all of them were making it up? That's beyond reason.

There's still more. The New Testament reports that over five hundred saw Him, after He had risen from the dead.[3] The resurrection of Jesus does not rest on some mysterious visions at dusk to a handful of impressionable dodos. These are historic happenings, occurring a number of times on varying occasions, and the Christians who report them are certain that they have seen and touched the Man who came back from the dead. They were there.

Let me ask you a question. Do you know any Jews? Are they by and large gullible people? Do you consider them naive dupes? Are they the types who will readily swallow a story? Or isn't it the exact opposite? Aren't they mostly "from Missouri"? Don't you have to show them? Not just once, but many times. They demand evidence before they will believe your story.

Look, I ought to know. I was brought up as an ethical Jew with hardly any religion. Before I believed in Jesus, which happened in my early twenties, I had to be shown. I had to be convinced. In fact, I took the long way around. I first investigated every other religion in the world. Only reluctantly did I approach Christianity, probably because I had experienced some persecution from the so-called Christian world.

When I advanced nearer to Christianity it was the

110

resurrection which caused me to stumble. I found it not only difficult, but practically impossible to accept. However, I had learned that no other religion of man presented a Saviour who died for the sin of the world and rose from the dead. Christianity stands singular.

So, whichever way you look at it, you have to reckon with more than five hundred practical Jews who testify that they have seen—actually, bodily seen—the risen Jesus. If you want facts, here's a very obvious one.

"Did they see a vision, a ghost? It could hardly have been real. You don't mean to say they saw a body? I still think it was a hallucination."

I knew you would bring that up about ghosts. That's why I mentioned those five hundred witnesses. What would you call this? Mass hypnosis? Mass hallucination? Is that likely?

It so happens that you're not the first to raise this objection. The disciples themselves mentioned it. Luke records it in his Gospel, and as a doctor (which he was) he would be certainly most careful to gather the facts about spirits or actual bodies!

"They shrank back in terror, for they thought they were seeing a ghost." Now there's an honest admission. The disciples didn't believe it themselves, so they came up with this ghost theory.

" 'Why are you so worried?' said Jesus, 'and why do doubts arise in your minds? Look at my hands and my feet—it is really I myself! Feel me and see; ghosts have no flesh or bones as you can see that I have.' "

You can't get much plainer than this! But they still did not believe Him. They thought they were seeing things, and they were.

"But while they still could not believe it through sheer joy, and were quite bewildered, Jesus said to them, 'Have you anything here to eat?' They gave him

111

a piece of broiled fish and part of a honeycomb, which he took and ate in front of their eyes."[4]

Whoever heard of a ghost *eating?* When you finish your reading of these accounts, you come away convinced that no one made them up. It's not the sort of thing people make up. From all you know of the honesty and factual mind of the Jew, this cannot be a piece of invented nonsense. It's either in the realm of a fairy tale, or it *is* truth. And when later they preach about the resurrection, there's nothing about visions or ghosts.

"Do you really expect me to swallow this? Do you really think you can convince me? How can I just accept this resurrection bit? It's too much to ask."

It was too much for the disciples too. Their reaction was one of unbelief, when the women first broke the news. When Jesus Himself appeared, He "reproached them for their lack of faith and reluctance to believe. . . ."[5]

You've heard of doubting Thomas, haven't you? Well, the original doubting Thomas, one of the apostles, didn't believe his friends' story when they told him they had seen the risen Jesus. Thomas was absent on that first Easter and his reaction was violent: "Unless I see in his own hands the mark of the nails, and put my finger where the nails were, and put my hand into his side, I will never believe!"

Then a week later, "the disciples were indoors again and Thomas was with them. The doors were shut, but Jesus came and stood in the middle of them and said . . . to Thomas, 'Put your finger here—look, here are my hands. Take your hand and put it in my side. You must not doubt, but believe.' "

How had Jesus known? How would Thomas react now? He didn't touch the wounds. He didn't have to. He cried out: "My Lord and my God!"[6]

Doubting Thomas? Hardly. He becomes a man of

faith—real faith—faith that will carry him through to the rest of his life as he serves God. "There lives more faith in honest doubt, believe me, than in half the creeds," wrote Tennyson.[7]

"Well, if I'd been there," you say, "maybe I'd have believed it too. But I didn't have that advantage. Thomas was privileged. He saw. It doesn't seem quite fair. It's difficult just to believe."

Jesus anticipated that. He said to Thomas: "Is it because you have seen me that you believe? . . . Happy are those who have never seen me and yet have believed."[8]

I sympathize with your point of view, but I don't agree with your argument. You seem to think that seeing is believing. That's not so. Plenty of people saw the miracles of Jesus. They did not become believers. Even the religious leaders admitted that Jesus cured and healed many, but that did not make Christians of them.

Why not? Because believing leads to seeing. Simple faith transforms life. It's not the other way around. The woman who touched Jesus in the crowd had faith to be healed. That's why she was. Believing leads to seeing.

I'll sum it up in one sentence: *If Jesus had not risen from the dead, Christianity would not exist today.* It really comes down to that.

There are enough facts to substantiate the resurrection of Jesus. Over five hundred witnesses! And yet, unless you're willing to come humbly in faith, you'll never know whether Christ is alive.

Notes

[1]John 14:19,3
[2]Acts 2:24
[3]I Corinthians 15:6
[4]Luke 24:37–43
[5]Mark 16:14
[6]John 20:25–28
[7]*In Memoriam*
[8]John 20:29

CHAPTER 15

So—What's the Purpose of Life?

And now you ask me perhaps the most probing question of all: "What's the purpose of life? What's it all for? What's the point?"

Let me begin with something that may seem very remote. A physicist says that an electron is a little particle. Then he corrects himself and adds that it isn't always a particle. Sometimes it's like a wave, and they are very different. A particle is right there. It zips through a Geiger counter and you can record it. A wave is everywhere and spreads all over.

An electron is both particle and wave, which is a contradiction. But it's not that mysterious. It just depends on the way you look at it. Now, here's the clincher: "Actually the electron is *different* from either a particle or a wave," says the scientist! We are limited in our description of what happens inside an atom. Human language, he explains, can't describe it.

Why did I bring that up? Well, when you ask me about the purpose of life, I find myself somewhat like that physicist with some definitive phrases, but actually groping for language to describe it. Why? Because purpose is a personal thing, and it's elusive.

But I can identify with your question. I know what you mean. And since people don't discuss subjects which bore them, I realize your concern.

Beauty fades. Our health gets worse. We aren't spared misery or sorrow. We may blow up the world any day, and we live with an underground fear all the time. Is there anything that won't be snatched from us at the end? Is there anything that can outlast time itself? These are the questions that haunt us.

And this is precisely the time we need to ask ourselves as we do when we go out to the movies: "What's playing?" What's playing in my life? What's going on? And who's directing it? Is this just a light comedy to perk me up for a little while? Or is it a tragedy with no solution?

"Yes, that's my question," you say. "We live and we die. What for? I wonder about this. What's the point? It all seems so futile, so pointless at times."

Surely you are not the first to raise this question, are you? Don't you suppose that most rational people have pondered this by the time they reach forty—or should I say twenty-five? The renowned minister and counsellor, John Sutherland Bonnell, says that everyone who has reached the age of twenty-one has thought about suicide. So even then we've already bumped into the meaninglessness of life. . . .

Have you had the experience of walking through a museum, looking at those prehistoric mammals, the mummies from Egypt or even relics from early American times, and then you tell yourself that you'll be a corpse too, all too soon? You shake off that thought. You don't like thinking about it. It's such a bitter pill to swallow for the living.

"Life's but a walking shadow, a poor player
That struts and frets his hour upon the stage
And then is heard no more."[1]

I suppose this is all so very frustrating for modern man since he has pinned his hopes to evolution. I don't mean evolution as it relates to creation, but the evolution of the human race, man's evolving. Most moderns believe that we are improving. As the world gets older, man gets better, learns more, becomes more mature. Everything improves.

But it doesn't. Instead, the same old problems persist. In fact, they seem more unsolvable. Man's inhumanity to man remains. He doesn't use a club any more when he kills. He uses gas. He doesn't do it as crudely as the ancients. He does it most efficiently with atomic power.

And we find ourselves in another bind. We live in this scientific era, in which we aren't really asking ultimate questions any longer. We don't go around raising problems which science cannot answer. We generally dismiss these questions about the meaning of life. We simply shove them away.

But where can we shove them? What can we do with them? Isn't it precisely this suppression of meaning which bursts out from modern man's insides in all the futility, despair and boredom? Isn't it precisely this which drives him to his endless but empty pursuits of materialism and fun? This is the "now" generation, which means that we'd better get our kicks today. There may be no tomorrow.

It almost seems as if the good life has become a

116

compulsion. We owe it to ourselves to live big. That's our philosophy because we have lost the true meaning of life. We waste time because we don't know what time is for! We drift aimlessly because we haven't any goal. That's why Arthur Compton, Nobel prize winner in atomic physics, has said: "Science has created a world in which Christianity is a necessity."

"But can Christianity answer this question? Does Christianity give man a purpose?"

One way to find the Christian perspective is to consider what your alternatives are. You could be scientific and stop looking for ultimate answers. You have to take life as it comes, live it out, live with the futility, the boredom, the despair. Make your bed and lie in it. That's the way of the French existentialist Jean-Paul Sartre. "I find that I'm alive and it sickens me," he muses. There is no exit from the human dilemma. You are in a room without doors. That's life. And that, according to Sartre, is also hell. No exit.

You have another alternative. You can attempt some explanations. You can become an idealist, a philosopher, a pantheist, *anything* for that matter. You can explain the purpose of life with lovely words, words that smell like flowers at a funeral, covering up the cold stench of decay. Beautiful phrases like: God is all. God is everything. There is no evil. There is no death. You are eternal. Become conscious of the Divine. You are one with God. You are God. And so on.

But if these platitudes do not suit you, you can become a realist. You face the question. You think it through. You're made to think. Don't evade it. Let me ask you this: "What do you want most out of life?"

"I suppose I'd say, to be happy. I just want to be happy."

What if you're not happy?

"Then I have to find out how to become happy. Is

117

that the purpose of life? Is that the Christian answer? Happiness?"

Certainly the purpose of life is not to be unhappy! Some Christians create that impression. They seem to make you think that the world knows how to be happy and they've a command: "Thou shalt not be happy." As if Christians should feel guilty about having a good time. That's nonsense, of course.

But what is happiness? For some this means moving around, being on the go. Doing it with the group. Really swinging. If they stop, trouble arises. Then they're afraid. They become depressed. They may even have a breakdown. At least they have to think. And that means trouble.

Blaise Pascal says: "The king is surrounded by persons whose only thought is to divert the king, and to prevent his thinking of himself. For he is unhappy, king though he be, if he thinks of himself!" We are all like little kings, who keep busy and divert ourselves, in order to avoid the real issues.

Activity is not meaning. You can only find God in stillness. Activity cannot create happiness either. You need direction more than a merry-go-round of go, go, go.

When Jesus opened the Sermon on the Mount, He spoke about happiness. "Blessed are the poor in spirit . . . blessed are the meek . . . blessed are the pure in heart." This is how the Authorized Version has it. We usually read "blessed" with a halo over it. But it isn't so.

What Jesus was actually talking about was happiness. Inner happiness. Real happiness. Much to our surprise, however, what He tells us about happiness is completely opposite of what we've always thought.

Instead of saying, "happy are the rich," He says, "happy are the poor."

Instead of saying, "happy are the successful," He says, "happy are they who hunger and thirst for God."

Instead of saying, "happy are the happy," He concludes, "happy are the persecuted and sorrowing."

Is this realistic? You see, it's precisely those who are suffering, poor, hungry, miserable and in trouble who want to find out about meaning! The full are full. The empty want to be filled. Those who have a void seek for God. For more penetration on the meaning of happiness, you will need to meditate far more on the Sermon on the Mount.

But let's approach it from another point of view. We've been thinking of the purpose of life for what *we* can get out of it. Turn it around. Life is *given* to you. The moment you accept that life is a gift, you don't keep on asking, "Why was I born?" You dismiss that question. And you become a Christian realist.

Since you no longer ask what it's all about, you accept the fact that you are born. You're here. You came from the hand of God. You will return to God. Now what are you going to do about it? What are you going to make of your life? That's the burning issue. That's the real challenge. Since you're here, what does it all add up to? How can you live meaningfully?

"But I've been asking that all along. You're not giving me any concrete answers."

Perhaps you didn't get the force of my words. Life is a gift. What does this mean? Where did our life come from? From our parents? Yes, certainly. But actually it came from God. God is the Creator of life. God has given us life. God has made you, just as surely as He made the first man.

If, then, you are to find a purpose for life, you need to relate to God. You need to discover meaning by seeking God, responding to God.

It may interest you to know (in case you are not

119

aware of it) that one man in the field of psychiatry has founded his whole school on this truth. He has rejected Freud, Adler and others and bases his understanding of man on what he calls *logotherapy*. That refers (loosely translated) to the meaning of life. Man is in search of meaning. According to Dr. Viktor Frankl, man *must* discover meaning to remain alive.

Dr. Frankl endured the harrowing experiences of the Nazi concentration camps. Here he found for himself, while living at the edge of death, that the only thread to life was meaning. In our factual, scientific and highly skilled era, man is "that being who has entered the gas chambers upright, with the Lord's Prayer or the Shema Yisrael on his lips."[2]

As a Christian, what gives me meaning is God's entry into the world. He lived in our midst, died on a cross and rose from the dead. He is no distant and disinterested Creator, but the loving, compassionate God who has become one of us. This gives me reason for being!

"I know Christianity says, 'seek and you will find,' but I haven't found," you say. "And I think I've been seeking. How then can I discover the purpose for my life? Have you discovered the purpose for your life?"

Maybe this illustration will help. Have you ever met a person who has lived most of his life (if not all) in a small town? He was probably very provincial, wasn't he? Narrow-minded. Now, the world is like a small town. We've got it all fixed up real nice with modern conveniences, and we just don't want to leave it. Besides, we insist that there isn't anything else beyond the edge of town. At one end of Main Street is the hospital where we entered life, and at the other the funeral parlor where it ends. Nothing beyond. We can't leave our little village. Not even in thought.

Purpose must lead *beyond* this life. Those who refuse to accept this, break themselves on the emptiness, futility and misery of this existence. A purpose is an ideal, a plan, an aim, a goal. Since we are creatures who came from God and who will return to Him, how can we discover meaning in any other way?

That's why life *only* takes on meaning when it is related to God, and more specifically to God's love in Christ. That shatters my futility and fears. Since God loves the world, He loves me. It's difficult to believe, simple though it sounds. But it is profoundly true. And I must add that since He loves me, He loves every person, the whole world.

Let's ask ourselves this. Did Jesus have a purpose in life? If so, what was it? He seemed to sum it up in one sentence: "Set your heart on his Kingdom and his goodness," and so seek first the Kingdom of God.³ This Kingdom means God's rule in our lives, or simply, God in our lives. And since *Jesus* came to live in our midst, that very fact gives us great hope. He believed this life was *worth* living!

Yes, we'd better think about purpose. It is no mere academic question. One day we may be confronted by Him with whom we have to do, and He may say to us: "You know, son, that was a wonderful performance you gave down there on the stage of the world. You were in the lights and you tried your best. But you missed the point! You played the wrong part. You didn't follow the script."

And then it may all have been for nothing. What a shame that would be to discover you built on the sand, and now your whole life comes tumbling down with a terrible crash.

"The Kingdom of Heaven is like a merchant searching for fine pearls. When he has found a single pearl of great value, he goes and sells all his possessions and buys it."⁴ Jesus says that the Kingdom (that is, the

121

meaning of life) is the most important thing, the great issue. But He points it right back to you!

What will you give to find purpose, He asks? How vitally will you seek *beyond* the limits of this village-world? Can you ignore this question? Pretend there is nothing to it? Or will it be worthy of your best effort?

It all points back to us, doesn't it? But, hopefully, we will find this pearl of infinite value, and so also the personal and eternal meaning of our lives.

Notes

[1]*MacBeth*, Act V, Scene 5
[2]Victor E. Frankl, *Man's Search for Meaning* (New York: Washington Square Press, Inc., 1966). Used by permission.
[3]Matthew 6:33
[4]Matthew 13:45,46

CHAPTER 16

Now It's Your Move

In the famous story *Quo Vadis* a young man falls in love with a beautiful Christian girl. She spurns his advances because he's a pagan. One night he secretly enters a Christian meeting in the catacombs and is caught up by the electric presence of God. He felt, so writes the author, "that if he wished to follow that teaching, he would have to place on a burning pile all his thought, habits and character, his whole nature up to that moment, burn them into ashes, and then fill himself with a life altogether different, an entirely new soul."

Christianity is more than a polite assent to a set of interesting propositions. It demands action, commitment, and involvement. That young man was right.

123

The time has come to draw our conversations to a close. I must say that I've enjoyed our talks. I've tried to give you honest answers whenever this was possible. But now I want to put it like this: it's your move!

We can always engage in more discussion. We can pursue other topics. But we are also brought to a point where we have to make a decision. And this is that time, the time for action. The Bible has an embarrassing way of putting the question to us: "Today if ye shall hear his voice, harden not your hearts. . . . Behold, now is the accepted time; behold, now is the day of salvation."[1]

I really think that you know enough to make your move. I don't think you want to fight any longer. You don't want to flee either. And you can't just forget it. Face it then. You have sufficient to act on. That's really all God asks of you. That's all He asks at any time.

We've touched on this before. "Follow Me," said Jesus. He meant for us to come and walk with Him. When Jesus gave this invitation He didn't insist that anyone sign a credal statement. He didn't draw up a list of doctrines for acceptance. He simply invited men to come with Him, announcing and choosing the Kingdom of God.

No, you don't have to accept any statement of faith. You don't have to believe all the dogmas, not even all those we've talked about in our conversations. In fact, you *can't* believe them, can you? How can you force yourself to believe something you *don't* believe? That leaves only one road open—the road of experimentation and venture. It's like when you're going to buy a new car. The dealer suggests you step behind the wheel and test drive it. Take it out on the road. So—it's your move!

"But," you say, "there's a difference between a car and Christianity. You can see a car, handle it, feel it.

Not so Christianity. I can't see God. So, I don't know what you want me to do."

Of course there's a difference. But the principle remains the same.

A young fellow made a bargain with God: "I want to know if Christ is real," he said. "If He is, I'll give Him my life. If not, I want to forget all about it." That seemed fair enough. But this was his stipulation: it would only be real if he could love his father.

Every day his father drove him home from the factory, and every day he'd lecture George. He told George to work harder, to apply himself more. As his father talked on, George boiled over with resentments. If Christianity is for real, George wanted a new attitude toward his father.

I wish I could tell you exactly what took place, but I can't. A week later everything was changing. Maybe George changed. Maybe his father. At least the lectures stopped and the resentments disappeared. The upshot of it all was that George was convinced Christianity worked!

You can test the reality of Christ. Of course He will reveal Himself in some other way to you. But there's always one place in your life where God can take hold, and, one place where you can begin to trust Him, too. Can you make that experiment? Is it a legitimate experiment? That's the question. Then if God is true, it'll work. If not, it won't.

"Try it," said Coleridge. "Don't talk to me of the evidences for Christianity. Try it." I want to add, *"and start where you are."* Of course, you can't really start any other place! The point is that you don't have to get better or know more. If Jesus invites you to follow Him, come now.

"But I'd like to keep an open mind. I'm not for this decision bit."

125

You realize, don't you, that a mind open at both ends is like a tunnel. The traffic comes in, drives through and proceeds out again. You've got to close your mind on something—on truth, for instance. Always keep it open for more truth, but close it on that reality which is given to you.

When you are confronted with a choice, to make no choice is the worst choice. If you don't plant flowers, you choose weeds, don't you? "The hottest places in hell," wrote Dante in another era, "are reserved for those who, in a period of moral crisis, maintain their neutrality." That was his point, not actually about hell, but indecision.

One other thing. You shouldn't look for a mystical experience, something emotional. Some people lead you to believe that unless you weep your eyes out, you won't become a Christian. There's a story about an old-timer who complained that young people "find Christ" too quickly. "I had to take eight trips to the altar before I was saved," he said. "But you were an exceptionally hard case," commented a friend, subtly. "The Lord doesn't have that much trouble with most people."

Instead of seeking an experience, seek God. And desire to do His will. "If anyone wants to do God's will, he will know whether my teaching is from God or whether I merely speak on my own authority,"[2] said Jesus.

That's an experiment. It is as though Jesus asks, why not try My way of living? Why not see if it is so? What do you have to lose? "Everyone then who hears these words of mine and puts them into practice is like a sensible man who builds his house on the rock."[3] The sensible man does something. He builds his life wisely.

I'm reminded of something a gambler once told me. "When there's a little money on the game," he said,

126

"we gamblers take it seriously. If there isn't, it's no fun. The more the better, of course."

Well, there's something at stake here. Everything, in fact. God or no God. Life or death. Heaven or hell. And you're playing for every cent you have. *Everything* to lose, and *everything* to gain! That's what it's all about!

"I've always heard preachers say, repent. You must repent. Repent of your sins and believe. I don't go for that either. Is this what you're trying to tell me—repent and believe?"

In a way I am, when I invite you to follow Jesus. That is repentance, turning your back on former goals and choosing God. A man with a severe emotional problem was sitting in the choir when suddenly during the sermon he felt led to say: "Lord, if this is the moment, I give up." And he did. That moment changed his life. He's a new person now.

That is repentance. To repent simply means to turn around and change directions.

Am I asking you to believe? Perhaps not in the sense that you must accept the doctrines of Christianity. You believe enough to approach God. You believe enough to seek Him. You believe enough to listen to Jesus. That's faith. Call it what you like. It leads to experience and new life.

"How did you become a Christian? Could you tell me how you were convinced?"

That's a big question you're asking. It took quite some time. I was raised without any religion as an ethical person. I had no formulated belief in God. I was an agnostic.

When I began to question the meaning of life, I proceeded to investigate various religions. Christianity came last on my list. It would be truer to say that Christianity wasn't on my list at all. But when I couldn't find what I was looking for anywhere else, I was challenged to consider Jesus. I rebelled against the person who challenged me. Very reluctantly and quite obstinately did I agree to examine Jesus.

I can't take you with me through that entire year of both searching and rebelling, questioning and running away. But I can tell you about the crucial moment, the moment that brought conversion. (Are you perhaps at that point now?) I came to the place where I was willing to go for broke. Call it "conviction of sin," a desperate feeling, or an awareness that something was missing. I went to a Christian whom I respected. I told him (bluntly) that I wanted to find out whether Christianity was true. I asked him to put it on the line, now. Now or never.

He gave me straight answers. He asked me three questions. I thought that I was ready for these, but I found that I wasn't. His first question was this:

"Do you believe that Jesus is the Son of God?" Did I, in fact, accept that Jesus is actually God in human flesh? I replied: "I don't believe that Jesus is the Son of God, but I'm willing to believe." I could not affirm it in words, and I knew that I had to be honest. All I could do was to express a willingness to believe.

Then he asked his second question: "Do you believe that Jesus died on the cross for you? Do you believe He took away your sins?"

I was caught. I had to reply in all honesty that I did not believe it, but again I added my willingness to believe. In other words, I was open. He didn't give me much indication whether I was passing or failing, but went on to question number three.

"Do you believe that Jesus rose again from the dead?" I was stumped, and I felt as though all this questioning would add up to a great big zero. I had heard about the resurrection, but I knew less about

128

Christianity than you do from our talks, so I said: "I don't believe it, but I'm willing to believe."

Let me interrupt here. You may think that I've reversed my field. I told you a moment ago that you had simply to follow Jesus and not to worry about doctrines. And now, in relating my own story, you note an emphasis on basic Christian beliefs. But it's not so different. He did *not* ask me to sign on a dotted line. I believed none of these doctrines, and I said so. Something else was at stake—my willingness!

This was *my* experiment. All that stood in my way was my obstinacy. My Christian friend wanted me to express my compliance. Didn't Jesus say that we had to become as little children to enter the Kingdom of Heaven? Humility.

Now he asked me to pray. He went down on his knees. So did my Christian wife, who was there. I had no choice, really. I prayed in the same way that I had talked with him.

It was the first time I'd been on my knees (and for me it meant being broken). It was the first time, too, I had prayed before other people. But in that definite, deliberate and unique moment the reality of Christ came over me. All I can tell you is that I passed from doubt to faith. My willingness to believe led to certainty.

Here is the key—in the simplicity of faith, in the denial of self, in the honesty of prayer. Humility opens a door. When you open that door, Christian living begins in a new dimension. "I stand knocking at the door. If anyone listens to my voice and opens the door, I will go into his house and dine with him, and he with me."[4]

It all began that day. Since then my life has been full of struggles, tests, failures and new beginnings, suffering and hope. But that is another story.

We've come to the starting line. That's where you

129

are. Jesus called it new birth. You can't force a birth. It has to happen to you, but you can be open.

So—it's your move.

Consider what will happen if you respond. A man enthused about his hobby of skin diving said to me: "If once you'd try it, you'd be hard to stop." If you really fall in love with a girl, your marriage will be hard to stop, too. Open the door of your being to Christ, and you'll be hard to stop as a Christian!

"Come to me all of you who are weary and overburdened and I will give you rest! . . . I will never refuse anyone who comes to me."[5] So urgently does Jesus, who died for us, invite us. Doesn't He deserve your "yes"?

It's your move.

Notes

[1]Hebrews 3:7,8;
 II Corinthians 6:2, KJV
[2]John 7:17

[3]Matthew 7:24
[4]Revelation 3:20
[5]Matthew 11:28; John 6:37

A Prayer

"Heavenly Father,
   If you are really there,
   If this is all true,
   If I can believe Jesus,
      I'm willing to come to You.
      I want to believe.
      I ask for forgiveness.
      I pray for new life.
      I need help.
Show me what You want of me.
Be with me in life's struggles.
Help me with my conflicts.
Let me actually do Your will in this world.
      So, if You are really listening,
      I ask You to hear my prayer
      Which I make in Jesus' name.
                              Amen."